# Teaching
## Students to Write

Argument
Essays That Define
Comparison/Contrast Essays
Personal Narratives
▶ **Research Reports**
Fictional Narratives

*The Dynamics of Writing Instruction series*

Peter Smagorinsky
Larry R. Johannessen
Elizabeth A. Kahn
Thomas M. McCann

HEINEMANN
Portsmouth, NH

**Heinemann**
361 Hanover Street
Portsmouth, NH 03801–3912
www.heinemann.com

*Offices and agents throughout the world*

The authors and publisher wish to thank those who have generously
given permission to reprint borrowed material:

Excerpts from "Of Mice and Men: The Dream of Commitment" in *John
Steinbeck's Re-Vision of America* by Louis Owens. Copyright © 1985. The
University of Georgia Press, Athens, Georgia. Reprinted by permission of
the Author's estate.

**Library of Congress Cataloging-in-Publication Data**
Teaching students to write research reports / Peter Smagorinsky . . . [et al.].
    p. cm. (The dynamics of teaching writing)
  Includes bibliographical references.
  ISBN-13: 978-0-325-03402-7
  ISBN-10: 0-325-03402-8
  1. English language—Composition and exercises—Study and
teaching (Middle school). 2. English language—Composition and
exercises—Study and teaching (Secondary). 3. Report writing—
Study and teaching (Middle school). 4. Report writing—Study and
teaching (Secondary). I. Smagorinsky, Peter.

LB1631.T333 2012
808'.0420712—dc23                      2011041652

Editors: Anita Gildea *and* Lisa Luedeke
Development editor: Alan Huisman
Production: Sonja S. Chapman
Cover design: Monica Ann Crigler
Typesetter: Valerie Levy / Drawing Board Studios
Manufacturing: Steve Bernier

Printed in the United States of America on acid-free paper

16  15  14  13  12  PAH  3  4  5

# CONTENTS

# Preface

Despite all the attention that writing instruction received during the last decades of the twentieth century, the teaching of writing in middle and high schools remains, at best, uneven. National Writing Project sites have conducted countless summer institutes, and new books about teaching writing appear routinely in publishers' catalogues. Yet assessments continue to find that students' writing is less accomplished than teachers might hope. Undoubtedly, the assessments themselves are not what they ought to be (Hillocks 2002). But even those with relatively good reputations, such as the National Assessment of Educational Progress, find that students in the United States are not writing as well as many people expect them to. What's going on here? And will yet another book about teaching writing make a difference?

We have written this series of small books in the hope that they will provide alternatives for teachers who are dissatisfied with teaching five-paragraph themes, traditional grammar lessons, and other form-driven writing approaches. This book employs what we call *structured process*, an approach developed by George Hillocks during his years as a middle school English teacher in Euclid, Ohio, during the 1960s. Hillocks and his students have researched this method and found it highly effective (Hillocks, Kahn, and Johannessen 1983; Smith 1989; Smagorinsky 1991; Lee 1993). In a more comprehensive research review, Hillocks (1986) found that over a twenty-year period, structured process writing instruction provided greater gains for student writers than did any other method of teaching writing.

We have also spent a collective 120-plus years using structured process instruction in our high school English classes. We do not claim to have discovered the one best way to teach writing; rather, our goal is to explain in detail a method that we all found successful in our teaching.

## What's in This Book? ·

A brief introduction explains why we believe it's important to teach students to do this kind of thinking and writing. Chapters 1 and 2 show you *how* to teach students to write research reports using structured process instruction; in them we describe classroom teaching strategies, provide a sequence of activities and handouts, and show examples of student work. Chapter 3 explains the structured process approach to teaching writing and its two main tenets, *environmental teaching* and *inquiry instruction*. This will help you understand why we designed the instruction modeled in this book the way we did; it will also help you design your own units of instruction in the future.

## What's in This Series?

There are six books, each following a similar format, each focusing on a different type of writing: research reports (the focus of this volume), personal narrative, fictional narrative, comparison/contrast essays, argument, and essays that define. If you find this book useful, you may want to consider reading the rest.

# Why Teach Students to Write Research Reports?

Most English/language arts curricula include a formal research paper at some point in middle and/or high school. While a few include some form of original research in which students design their own study or survey and gather their own data, most ask students to gather information from books, articles, Internet sources, and so forth and incorporate this material into a report that includes formal citations: works cited, references, or a bibliography.

The ability to comprehend, analyze, and synthesize facts, ideas, and concepts from a variety of sources and use proper forms of documentation is essential in formal education and in life. Larson (1988) even argues that writing the "junior theme" is an important bonding experience, a shared rite of passage. While writing a term paper, Larson found, students experience "a range of emotional states that are well out of their normal school experience. Many go through a process of personal involvement and self-searching that resembles an identity quest. As a result of the project students feel they have acquired a new status, one that separates them from the uninitiated and puts them closer to the status and power of an autonomous adult" (267).

According to the new common core standards, students need to be adept at gathering information, evaluating sources, and citing material accurately and be able to report findings from their research and analysis of sources in a clear and cogent manner. The Advanced Placement Language and Composition Exam requires students to synthesize information from a set of sources in order to create an original thesis and develop an argument.

Unfortunately, students often find it very difficult to analyze and synthesize material. They frequently end up pasting together a string of ideas that lacks focus and coherence and says little that is meaningful, insightful, or even comprehensible. Some educators suggest that the problem with research papers is that students write on remote or uninteresting topics and that better topics will produce better papers (Lamm 1998, among many other sources). Undoubtedly, writing on the assigned topic of how the skin color of sixteenth-century North African Muslims informs one's reading of *Othello, the Moor of Venice* might not inspire a student whose primary interest in life is repairing car engines. But simply providing ten thousand topics for research papers, as Lamm has done, is hardly a solution.

One way to help students avoid disengaged and uninspired research reporting is to have them focus on argumentation related to a topic they're interested in and include some original research in addition to gathering information from existing sources. This way, their inquiry advances their ability to persuade others of their beliefs, and they have a reason to seek additional information to support their views. As students construct arguments and find convincing evidence to support their position on an issue, they engage in critical thinking and are less likely simply to "paste together" information and quotations.

Students are often also asked to conduct research related to literature they are reading. Students reading Shakespeare's *Romeo and Juliet* may research the Globe Theater, Shakespeare's life, leisure activities in Elizabethan England, or life in Italy in the fifteenth century. Or students may analyze connections between a literary work and the author's life or the work's social or cultural milieu. Or they may interpret a text after examining articles written by literary critics. The "literary" research paper is particularly difficult for students because the sophistication and complexity of the sources often overwhelm them and leave them without a clear sense of direction or purpose. Focusing on argument can help with these problems.

Lessons for teaching argument are presented in another book in this series, *The Dynamics of Writing Instruction: Teaching Students to Write Argument.* A research paper may also incorporate comparisons/contrasts and extended definitions; these types of writing are addressed in other books in the series.

Whether it is an analysis and synthesis of original or previously gathered information, the ability to report on research is a skill needed to succeed in school and in life. The structured process approach is particularly effective in teaching students to write research reports.

# Teaching the Argumentation Research Report

One way to interest students in writing research reports is to focus on an issue that is being debated locally, nationally, or even internationally. Recently at Betsy's school, the rules were changed to allow students to use cell phones in the cafeteria during lunch periods. Previously, cell phones could be used only before or after school or in the classroom with the teacher's permission. Some students cheered the change, arguing that using cell phones in the cafeteria does no harm to learning and allows students to share their plans with their parents. Other students argued that students in classrooms would now surreptitiously text their friends in the cafeteria and vice versa. The school newspaper printed an editorial and letters to the editor, and local newspapers even published a few articles about the issue.

This is a perfect issue for students to research. They can find information about other schools' cell phone policies and their advantages and disadvantages. They can find studies about the positive and negative uses of cell phones in school. They can interview or survey students about their cell phone use in school (How many students have cell phones in school? Why do they have them? How often do they use their cell phone in the cafeteria? In the classroom? For what purposes?). They can interview or survey teachers about classroom interruptions or disturbances involving cell phones and the ways, if any, that they have students use cell phones for educational purposes. They can then use the results of their research to take a position on whether or not allowing cell phones in the school cafeteria is a good idea.

Even if there isn't a "hot" issue in the school or community, you can identify a real issue somewhere in the world that will interest your students. For example, perhaps a school is planning to randomly test students for alcohol use, or parents want to return their adopted child because he tried to burn down their house.

## Task Analysis

Our approach to an argumentation research paper is the one set out in Toulmin (1958) and Toulmin et al. (1984). Students:

- Take a position on an issue, stated as a *thesis*.

- Develop a series of *claims* (reasons, main points, etc.) in support of their position.

- Support *claims* with specific *data* or *evidence*.

- Include *warrants* to clarify the connection between the data (evidence) and the claim.

- Anticipate *counterarguments* or *counterevidence*.

- Respond to or *rebut* counterarguments or counterevidence.

They also present bibliographical citations in an accepted format.

So that research skills don't have to be taught at the outset, instruction begins with an activity based on an accessible topic about which students have strong opinions. The topic should also be controversial (i.e., it is *debatable* or *raises doubts*), so students, while arguing a thesis by means of claims, evidence, and warrants, can evaluate and respond to opposing claims and have their own thinking critiqued by others.

After an initial oral discussion, students express their opinions, claims, evidence, and warrants and rebut one another's claims in online, real-time written exchanges on an Internet "chat" site. Instruction relies first on generating ideas; later students identify the components of argument as they examine how they have stated, illustrated, warranted, and defended their beliefs.

During the lesson, students discuss controversial issues, argue for a credible and persuasive perspective, receive continual feedback on their thinking and writing, and develop criteria for assessment.

## Stage 1. Gateway Activity: Making a Strong Argument

**EPISODE 1.1.** Begin by debating a student on an inherently interesting and controversial topic: which team has the best chance of winning an upcoming local or national sports event, whether the school should ban MP3 players or cell phones, whether lunch periods in the cafeteria should be accompanied by music played by student DJs, whether students should be allowed off campus during the school day. Choose an outgoing, vocal student, and work out your respective positions before class (the rest of the students don't have to know that the argument has been staged, if not scripted). As an alternative, ask another teacher or an administrator to debate you.

**EPISODE 1.2.** Ask students to discuss what arguments were raised, which were strongest/weakest, and why. Ask them to identify what evidence, if any, was provided to support each person's claims. Your goal is to prompt students to develop criteria for what makes an argument effective and convincing. As students identify most of the relevant features, suggest the Toulmin terminology (*claim, evidence, warrants, counterarguments*).

Now tell students that these are the elements they will focus on as they write a research paper supporting their position on an issue. As an example, you might explore one claim from the previous discussion and label each feature:

*Overall thesis*: Students should not be allowed to have cell phones in the school building or on the school grounds.

*Claim 1*: Students are too undisciplined with their phones, and if they are allowed to have them at school, they will spend too much time calling, texting, searching the Internet, downloading and playing games, and doing other things that distract them from their schoolwork.

*Evidence*: During a single week, using cell phones, one student photographed other students relieving themselves in the washroom and posted the photos on the Internet; another photographed quiz questions early in the day and sent them to her friends taking the same class in a later period; another used the Internet to get test answers while taking an exam; and yet another arranged a drug deal in a school washroom.

*Warrant*: Even though cell phones may be used for legitimate purposes, such as contacting parents or calling 911 during an emergency, they are too often used for unethical purposes; therefore the overall effect of allowing cell phones in school is deleterious to students' academic attention and their moral conduct in school.

You might also look at counterarguments or counterevidence students have presented and consider how they could be responded to and/or rebutted:

*Counterargument:* In an emergency students can use a cell phone to tell their parents what is happening and whether they are safe.

*Response/rebuttal:* During emergencies, our school posts information for parents on the school website. This official information is more accurate and reliable than what students would be able to tell their parents on a cell phone. Therefore, cell phones are unnecessary for school emergencies.

## Stage 2. Introducing Research Writing

Research writing instruction often focuses on aspects of form: how to write a bibliographic entry in the standard form of choice, how to produce note cards (long after computers have provided alternatives), and so on. Teachers may also show students how to find trustworthy sources on the Internet, locate sources in encyclopedias and other print media, and otherwise locate information.

How to translate this information into a coherent report or argument gets less attention. As a result, students are always walking the fine line between reporting information found in a source and plagiarizing; knowing how to assemble the information they have gathered into a properly documented presentation in their own voice has baffled students for generations. When the thrust of the writing shifts from the information as an end in itself to an opinion based on that information, plagiarizing becomes less of an issue: students concentrate on fashioning the information into evidence.

Begin by having students develop a position on an issue and gather evidence to support their position. Introduce the use of sources by providing one article about an issue that will generate debate. Have students use information from this source to develop their own argument in their own voice.

**EPISODE 2.1.**  Hand out Figure 1–1, "Should Schools Test Students for Alcohol Use?" Have students read the information and discuss whether they think screening students for alcohol use is a good idea. Have students use a graphic organizer like the one in Figure 1–2 to identify arguments and evidence that could be used by those in favor of the test and those against it. Encourage students to include evidence based on their own experience or obtained from other sources. (Students could also blog about the issue.) Point out effective examples of evidence, warrants, rebuttal, and so forth. Examples of claims that lack supporting evidence or that need a warrant may also be valuable.

**EPISODE 2.2.**  Have students use Figure 1–3 to plan and then draft their argument about whether alcohol screening by schools is a good idea or should not be done.

**EPISODE 2.3.**  Have students, in small groups, review their drafts (hard copies or computer files) in class. (If students are using hard copies, they'll need highlighters.) For each paper, students first identify the position (thesis) of the writer. Next they highlight each of the claims made by the writer in support of the position (thesis). For each claim, students evaluate whether the writer has provided supporting evidence and a warrant. They should also address whether

**Figure 1–1.** Should Schools Test Students for Alcohol Use?

[This information is from a *USA Today* article, "School's Test Can Detect Alcohol Use 3 Days Prior," by Charisse Jones, March 4, 2007, online.]

In addition to drug testing, a high school in New Jersey requires randomly selected students to undergo a screening that can detect whether they drank alcohol up to 80 hours before. The test detects ethyl glucuronide (EtG), an indicator of alcohol consumption that is found in urine. It is a recent addition to alcohol and drug screens being used in school systems around the USA.

All students who are involved in extracurricular activities and sports or have privileges such as being able to park on campus are given the EtG test, which is about 75 percent of the students. On any given day, around five to ten students are randomly selected to undergo a drug test or EtG screen.

According to the school's superintendent, students are not punished based on the EtG test. "There is no loss of privileges," he says. "Our counselors talk to the children about the dangers of drugs and alcohol, and we communicate with Mom and Dad, saying we believe their child may have been drinking."

Although Ed Barocas, legal director of the ACLU of New Jersey, understands the desire to keep students away from alcohol and other drugs, he thinks that it is a problem if this concern overtakes other legitimate concerns including protecting families' rights to privacy and teaching students that our justice system is built on the concept of innocent until proven guilty, not the other way around.

Marsha Rosenbaum of the New York–based Drug Policy Alliance says there are more effective strategies, such as after-school activities for students, better drug education in high schools, and counseling. She says that if parents want to test their children they can easily purchase drug tests at a neighborhood drug store. They don't need the school to do this.

The school's principal says that for students facing peer pressure, drug and alcohol testing "gives them an out. If they're at a party and someone says, 'Do you want to try this or that,' they can easily say, 'I don't want to risk my participation [in sports].'"

**Figure 1–2.** Examining Different Viewpoints on an Issue

*Is administering an EtG screening to test students for alcohol use a good idea?*

| Yes | No |
| --- | --- |
| | |
| | |
| | |
| | |
| | |
| | |
| | |
| | |

**Figure 1–3.** Planning for Writing

A school in New Jersey is testing students using EtG screening for alcohol use. Is this a good idea?

*What is your position on this issue (thesis)?*

*What is the strongest point (claim) in favor of your position?*

*What evidence can you provide to support this claim?*

*What is your warrant (how or why does the evidence support the claim)?*

*What evidence might someone on the other side present against your claim? Explain.*

*How do you counter (argue against) this point or evidence? Explain.*

*What is another point (claim) that you want to make in support of your position?*

*What evidence can you provide to support this claim?*

**Figure 1–3.** Planning for Writing (*continued*)

*What is your warrant (how or why does the evidence support the claim)?*

*What evidence might someone on the other side present against your claim? Explain.*

*How do you counter (argue against) this point or evidence? Explain.*

*What additional point (claim) can you make in favor of your position? Or what point (claim) does the other side make that you disagree with?*

*What is your evidence?*

*What is your warrant?*

the writer has anticipated and responded to the major arguments on the other side of the issue. Notes to the writer are made directly on the papers.

**EPISODE 2.4.**  Discuss appropriate ways to document information from sources, which can range from informal to formal. When using only one (or a limited number) of sources, writers might indicate the source of the information directly in the text—for example,

In a *USA Today* article, "School's Test Can Detect Alcohol Use 3 Days Prior" (March 4, 2007), Charisse Jones explains that on any

**Figure 1–4.** Rubric for Evaluating Research Writing

| | 1 | 2 | 3 | 4 |
|---|---|---|---|---|
| *Statement of position* | Position may not be clear throughout or may not be maintained. | Position is mostly clear and mostly maintained throughout. | Position is clear and maintained throughout. | Position is clear and effectively stated or implied. The focus is sharp throughout. |
| *Use of claims (points) to develop the argument* | The "argument" is merely a list of claims without support or development. | There are a number of claims with some minimal supporting evidence. | Most claims develop the argument and are supported with evidence. | Claims are effective in developing the argument and are supported with evidence. |
| *Use of evidence and warrants* | Almost no evidence is provided. | Some evidence is provided but is limited, incomplete, or repetitious. Warrants are missing or minimal. | Evidence is adequate and usually specific. Sometimes warrants are included. | Ample specific, effective evidence is included. Warrants effectively link evidence and claims. |
| *Response to counterarguments and/ or counterevidence* | There is little or no recognition of counterarguments and/or counterevidence. | Counterarguments and/or counterevidence may be acknowledged, but the development and/or response is brief or unclear. | Counterarguments and/or counterevidence are recognized, and there is some response to them. | Counterarguments and/or counterevidence are addressed effectively. |
| *Organization* | Organization is confusing or ineffective. Composition is without a discernable beginning, middle, or end. Transitions and linking expressions are missing. | Organization is discernable with an introduction, body, and conclusion. Transitions and linking expressions are weak. | Introduction, body, and conclusion are adequate. Organization is clear. Some transitions and linking expressions are used. | Introduction, body, and conclusion are effective. Organization is clear and logical. Linking expressions and transitions are smooth and effective. |

**Figure 1–4.** Rubric for Evaluating Research Writing (*continued*)

| | | | | |
|---|---|---|---|---|
| *Proofreading* | Many major errors in conventions often interfere with understanding. | Some major errors and many minor errors in standard conventions occasionally interfere with understanding. | There are some errors in standard conventions, but they do not impede understanding. | There are few errors in standard conventions. |
| *Documentation of sources* | Information from sources is rarely, if ever, cited appropriately. | Some information from sources is cited appropriately. | Most information from sources is cited appropriately. | All information from sources is cited appropriately. |

given day, around five to ten students are randomly selected to undergo a drug test or EtG screen.

More formal is to provide a parenthetical citation—(Jones online)—and a works cited page with a complete bibliographic entry:

Jones, Charisse. "School's Test Can Detect Alcohol Use 3 Days Prior." *USA Today* 4 March 2007.

For formal research reports with a number of sources, writers are more likely to provide internal, parenthetical citations and a works cited or references page at the end of the paper. Let students know what approach you want them to use in writing this paper.

**EPISODE 2.5.**  After students have revised their drafts based on the feedback from their peers, evaluate students' final papers in relation to the characteristics of effective argument that have been the focus of instruction. You and your students could create a rubric similar to the one in Figure 1–4. Post the students' writing in the classroom, in a school display case, or on a website for others to read.

**EPISODE 2.6.**  If students need additional practice, use the information in Figure 1–5. Have students debate and write about whether it is a good idea for schools to implement a four-day school week (by extending each school day and having one day off) in order to save money. Follow the process described in Episodes 2.1 through 2.5, or have students work independently.

**Figure 1–5.** The Four-Day School Week

*[From "Research Brief: A Review of the Evidence on the Four-Day School Week," prepared by Christine Donis-Keller and David L. Silvernail of the Center for Education Policy, Applied Research and Evaluation, University of Southern Maine, February 2009.]*

With schools facing budget shortfalls, some schools are saving money in transportation, facilities, and personnel costs by reducing the number of days students attend classes. The school day is extended each of the four days so that students attend school the same number of hours during four days that they would during five days.

Currently, around 120 school districts across the country are implementing a four-day school week. Most school districts take either Monday or Friday off.

Researchers report that schools with four-day weeks have saved on utilities, food service, school buses, and long-term wear and tear on facilities. They have also found that pay for substitute teachers has decreased because of reduced teacher absences. Savings range from two to nine percent of a school district's operating budget.

In a study of New Mexico's four-day schools, researchers found that students' achievement did not suffer, and in some districts it improved. A study of five rural Colorado school districts found that the change in schedule had no discernable impact on test performance. Several studies have found that the four-day week has resulted in increased attendance for both teachers and students.

Some parents complain about having to find and pay for childcare for the day that students are not in school. Some students are concerned that they become too fatigued with the longer school day and are less productive in classes and athletics.

## Stage 3. **Researching an Issue**

Students strengthen their arguments by gathering information from many sources. This helps them argue more effectively with their peers about topics they care about.

**EPISODE 3.1.** Introduce an issue currently in the news, such as the role of schools in making sure that students eat healthy foods. Should middle and high schools sell junk food in the cafeteria, in vending machines, and/or at athletic events on school property? Should all junk food be eliminated from middle and high schools? Explain to students that together you will focus on this issue in the context of learning how to write a research paper.

Spend some time defining and illustrating types of "unhealthy food" or "junk food" found in or near many schools. For example:

- free and reduced-price breakfasts that consist of pancakes made with white flour, sugar, and salt and served with oleo-margarine and sugar-based syrup, or cereals made from processed flour that are high in sugar and calories

- vending-machine potato chips, corn chips, candy bars, sugary soft drinks, and similar products

- cheeseburgers, french fries, slices of cake and pie, sugar-based beverages, string beans that have been cooked into limp strands of vitamin-depleted mush, and other unhealthy food

- shops near the school grounds that sell ice cream, fast food, unhealthy snacks, and similar fare.

This discussion needn't be as involved as one related to an essay that defines, but it should at least try to distinguish what is and what is not junk food. For example, you could identify all the food available in the school and classify it as junk food or not, the criteria for a definition emerging as the students compare and contrast the various products. Another option is to begin with a formal definition of junk food from an authoritative source.

Alternatively, you could have students grapple with the junk food problem in small groups (which allows greater participation) and follow it with a whole-class discussion. Having students generate definitions inductively in small groups allows them to own their definitions and classifications, but this more time-consuming approach might not fit your schedule.

You could also ask students to research the food served in the school's cafeteria and vending machines:

- Find out what food is available.

- Categorize the food available as either junk food or healthy food.

- Observe five different (unnamed) students during lunch, list what each student is eating, and categorize each item as junk food or healthy food.

Ask students to bring their notes to class, and then have them compile the results.

**EPISODE 3.2.**   Hand out Figure 1–6 and ask the students to read it. Alternatively, either on your own or with the students' help, gather several articles containing credible information on the issue for them to read. Then have your students, in small groups, use a chart similar to the one in Figure 1–7 to summarize the arguments and evidence that can be or have been raised on both sides of the issue. Finally, have students, as a class, share the information on their charts.

**EPISODE 3.3.**   By now, students may realize they do not have the support they need to develop and defend their positions. Give them the opportunity to find more printed material and Internet sources dealing with the issue of junk food and the role of school as an educational institution. (You might reserve time in the school library or media center.) Remind students how to document these sources so they can include them in their bibliography or list of references.

**EPISODE 3.4.**   If possible, have students blog or "chat" (on blogger .com or edmodo.com, for example) about whether schools should eliminate junk food. Remind them to provide evidence for their claims and counterarguments. You can participate as well until

**Figure 1–6.** Information About Junk Food in Schools

**Aptos Middle School**

Beginning in January, 2003, Aptos Middle School, in the San Francisco Unified School District, replaced junk food in the cafeteria with healthy choices. Soda, chips, mega-colossal burgers (58 percent fat), chicken wings (61 percent fat), and hot dogs (77 percent fat) were eliminated.

Students were surveyed about their favorite healthy choices, and based on the results items such as sushi, deli sandwiches, baked chicken with rice, freshly made soup, salads, and fruit desserts were added. All drinks with added sugar were removed, including those in vending machines. Only 100 percent fruit juices, water, and milk are now available.

Dana Woldow, chair of the Aptos PTSA Student Nutrition Committee explained, "We tried to make sure that every choice we offered contained nutrients, not just empty calories. . . . It is not enough that our food be less bad for the kids. We want the food to be good for them. Our turkey and roast beef sandwiches are made with lots of fresh lettuce and tomato. The homemade soups are loaded with vegetables."

Converting to healthy food choices has increased the profits of Aptos's food service from losing money in 2002 to finishing 2003 more than $6,000 in the black. Aptos (860 students) made more than $2,000 in May 2003, while A. P. Giannini (1,280 students), which still sells soda and junk food, made less than $90 for the month.

Teachers and administrators report that eliminating junk food significantly improved student behavior after lunch and reduced litter. Parents feel less pressure to pack their kids' lunches every day because they know their children will not be tempted to spend their lunch money on poor food choices.

"Junk Food Out, Profits In at San Francisco Middle School,"
July 13, 2003, website of Parents Advocating School Accountability,
San Francisco (www.pasasf.org)

*(continues)*

**Figure 1–6.** Information About Junk Food in Schools (*continued*)

### Childhood Obesity

1976–1980: 6.5% of 6–11-year-olds and 5.0% of 12–19-year-olds are overweight.

1988–1994: 11.3% of 6–11-year-olds and 10.5% of 12–19-year-olds are overweight.

1999–2000: 15.1% of 6–11-year-olds and 14.8% of 12–19-year-olds are overweight.

2003–2004: 18.8% of 6–11-year-olds and 17.4% of 12–19-year-olds are overweight.

> From the National Health and Nutrition Examination Survey conducted by the Centers for Disease Control and Prevention. Source: National Center for Health Statistics. Found in "Update: Junk Food in Schools," in *Issues & Controversies on File,* Facts on File News Services, March 23, 2007, www.2facts.com

### Vending Machines

Vending machines with junk food are a significant source of money for many schools, generating more than $750 million each year. In 2000, High Point High School made nearly $100,000 from vending machines in the school. That amount was about 25% of the school's operating budget. William Ryan, principal of High Point High School, in Prince George's County, Maryland, says, "This money is crucial. There are things that I do with that money around the school for the students that I could not do [without it]." With tight budgets and decreasing money from the government, schools often have to cut music, athletic, and art programs, as well as technology and library resources.

> From "Junk Food in Schools," January 24, 2007, *Issues & Controversies on File,* Facts on File News Services, www.2facts.com

**Figure 1–6.** Information About Junk Food in Schools (*continued*)

### Berkeley, California, Public Schools

A well-respected chef, Ann Cooper, was brought in to make changes in the cafeterias of 16 of Berkeley's public schools. She introduced whole-wheat veggie pizza with toppings like zucchini, blue cheese, and walnuts, but trash cans were filled with uneaten slices. More than 200 students signed a petition protesting the pizza and other new offerings. In her first year, Cooper went tens of thousands of dollars over budget and lost many students as customers.

From "Slow Food Movement," by Sarah Glazer, in
*CQ Researcher*, Volume 17, January 26, 2007, pages 73–96,
http://library.cqpress.com/cqresearcher/cqresrre2007012600

### Naperville, Illinois, Middle and High Schools

Schools in Naperville District 203 resemble health clubs, with heart monitors, treadmills, stair-steppers, and even a rock-climbing wall. According to Phil Lawler, physical education coordinator, "instead of teaching sports skills," gym classes focus on "health, wellness, and lifestyle. So many are pointing the finger at poor nutrition, but a bigger factor is kids are just not physically active. Physical education for every kid in school could be the solution to get control of health care." While running laps, students are scored on their performances within their own heart zones, not on how well they compete against others. Student cholesterol tests have improved every year since testing began in 1994. Fitness tests also show gains, with only 3 percent of Naperville ninth-graders considered overweight.

From "The Shape We're In: Innovative Schools Teach Lifelong Health
by Just Saying No to Status Quo," by Lorna Collier,
*Philadelphia Inquirer*, May 27, 2003, SIRS Knowledge Source,
http://sks.sirs.com

**Figure 1–7.** Should Middle Schools and High Schools Eliminate Junk Food Sales in the Cafeteria, in Vending Machines, and at Athletic Events?

| Yes | No |
| --- | --- |
|  |  |
|  |  |
|  |  |
|  |  |
|  |  |
|  |  |
|  |  |
|  |  |

students get the idea. For example, if Sam writes, "Students will simply stop eating the cafeteria food, and the school will lose money if no one buys lunches," you might respond, "Interesting point, Sam. Will they not eat anything at all in protest, or will they get food somewhere else?" Or if LaShae says, "It would help students who are overweight," you might respond, "LaShae, you say that eliminating junk food in the cafeteria would help students not be overweight. Can you explain more about why you think it would have this effect?" or, "LaShae, what about students who are in good physical shape and healthy? Is it fair to keep them from having junk food when they want it?" Your goal is to encourage students to expand their thinking, defend their claims, and address counterarguments. Your comments are also models of how they can respond to their classmates' comments.

After the blogging session, photocopy or project transcripts of the exchanges and ask students to identify strong arguments and evidence and effective points.

If your classroom is not equipped with computers, substitute a conventional classroom discussion. Although students' oral remarks are more ephemeral and harder to classify than their written comments, an oral exchange is similar and can be the basis of Episode 3.5.

**EPISODE 3.5.** Take elements of one of the previous arguments and label them clearly so that students understand what they need to accomplish when making a point. Here's an example:

*Overall thesis*: Junk food should not be available anywhere in the school because it contributes to the obesity and poor health of students and makes school a site for learning unhealthy habits.

*Claim 1*: Vending machines, while popular with students and a source of income for the school, primarily serve products that are high in sugar, salt, fat, chemicals, and other unhealthy ingredients.

*Evidence*: For example, the beef jerky sold in all the school vending machines contains beef parts, mechanically separated chicken parts, water, salt, corn syrup, flavorings, dextrose, spices, hydrolyzed corn gluten, soy and wheat gluten proteins, sodium nitrite, and lactic acid starter culture.

*Warrant*: These ingredients, which are typical of the processed foods found in vending machines, contribute to bad health. There are two sources of salt (table salt and sodium nitrite), which often elevates blood pressure, and two sources of sugar (corn syrup and dextrose), which makes people obese and can make students hyperactive. Hydrolyzed corn gluten is a source of monosodium glutamate (MSG), which in addition to providing yet more sodium, has been found in some studies to cause retinal degeneration and kill brain cells and may lead to behavior disorders, learning disabilities, reproductive disorders, obesity, irritable bowel syndrome, heart irregularities, asthma, and migraine headaches. Lactic acid starter culture is often based on milk and so is dangerous for sufferers of particular allergies.

*Counterargument and rebuttal*: Although there might be some beneficial protein in the beef and chicken parts, and although there are more of these ingredients than any other individual ingredient, on the whole this food, like other vending machine snacks, is detrimental to one's health and should be avoided. Simply including protein is not a good reason to sell a product if the protein source (especially beef) is implicated in heart disease. Producing beef also contributes to global warming by displacing vegetable farms with beef farms and their cattle, who consume additional vegetables that people might eat and produce flatulence that adds climate-warming methane gas to the atmosphere; beef farms are one of the world's greatest threats to climate stability.

Review this argument and emphasize that each claim needs to be clearly related to the main argumentative point, buttressed with evidence, and explained in terms of a warrant. When juxtaposed with an argument that supports the availability of junk food in the school, the strengths and weaknesses of the competing arguments can be evaluated relative to one another.

## Stage 4A. Language Lesson 1: Practicing Warrants

Students who have been taught to write primarily via five-paragraph themes may have little experience relating claims and evidence by means of warrants. Most instruction in expository writing focuses on generalization and support, terms that correspond to claims and evidence. But as Hillocks (2002) observes, the evidence produced in such a template may or may not make sense relative to the claim.

Students will produce stronger evidence for their claims and drive home their points more forcefully when they explain why or how the evidence supports their claims. Therefore, have them complete the exercise in Figure 1–8, in which they create warrants for given claims and evidence. If students are working with this element of argument for the first time, have them do the problems in pairs rather than individually.

**Figure 1–8.** Writing Warrants

Each of the following problems states a claim and then offers evidence to support it. For each pair of statements, provide a warrant that clearly explains why the evidence supports the claim. The claim is stated so that you may take either a pro (for) or con (against) position. Decide which position the evidence supports and, through your warrant, explain why.

**Example:**

*Claim*: Soft drinks are [are not] unhealthy because they contain a superabundance of sugar.

*Evidence*: One popular cola beverage is made according to the following recipe: 30 cups of sugar, 2 gallons of water, 1 quart of lime juice, 4 ounces of citrate of caffeine, 2 fluid ounces of citric acid, 1 ounce of extract of vanilla, 3/4 fluid ounce of extract of cola, and 3/4 fluid ounce of fluid extract of coca.

*(continues)*

**Figure 1–8.** Writing Warrants (*continued*)

> *Warrant*: Because there are 128 ounces of fluid in a gallon, there are 30 cups of sugar per each 256 ounces of water. Adding the remainder of the fluids produces a ratio of 30 cups of sugar in each 296.5 total ounces of fluid, or roughly 1 cup per each 10 ounces of total fluid. Therefore every 12-ounce can of this product includes roughly 1.2 cups of sugar. Because the amount of sugar in each can of the "regular" variety of this beverage is so thoroughly saturated with sugar, this product is likely to contribute to its consumer's obesity.

Either by yourself or with a partner, provide a warrant relating each of the following claims to the supporting evidence:

1. *Claim*: Potato chips are [are not] unhealthy because the way in which they are prepared is [is not] unhealthy for the human body.

   *Evidence*: Potato chips are made by slicing each potato into a thin oval and deep-frying it in vegetable oil, then adding salt and additional flavors.

   *Warrant*:


2. *Claim*: The pancakes served in the free and reduced-price breakfast program are [are not] detrimental to one's health.

   *Evidence*: The pancakes are made from processed flour, sugar, salt, eggs, and baking soda, and are served with butter and cane syrup.

   *Warrant*:

**Figure 1–8.** Writing Warrants (*continued*)

3. *Claim*: The sausages served in the free and reduced-price breakfast program should [should not] be considered junk food.

   *Evidence*: Inexpensive sausages of the sort served in these breakfasts contain up to 50% fat and have a salt content of 2–3%. They are additionally cured with salt and sodium nitrite, making them very salty. The meat itself comes from every part of the pig, meaning that a sausage may include bone remnants, intestines, internal organs, ground hooves, and other parts that few people would eat by choice.

   *Warrant*:

4. *Claim*: Removing junk food in vending machines will [will not] significantly reduce funds for important school programs.

   *Evidence*: According to one principal, her school now receives nearly $100,000 a year from vending machines. That money is used to pay for girls' and boys' volleyball teams, boys' and girls' cross country track teams, and girls' and boys' gymnastics teams.

   *Warrant*:

5. *Claim*: When healthy choices are available along with junk food, students will [will not] tend to select the healthy options.

   *Evidence*: On a typical day at River Grove High School, the lunch featured grilled chicken breasts, rice, steamed broccoli, and a fruit cup of fresh watermelon cubes. The cafeteria

(*continues*)

**Figure 1–8.** Writing Warrants (*continued*)

reported that 819 out of 1,120 students purchased this lunch selection, while the rest selected less healthy options.

*Warrant*:


6.  *Claim*: The ingredients in candy bars are [are not] unhealthy and make [do not make] it hard for students to concentrate and sit still during class.

    *Evidence*: One popular candy bar is made from water, corn syrup, butter, vanilla extract, peanut butter, salt, sugar, caramel, peanuts, and chocolate chips.

    *Warrant*:


7.  *Claim*: Pizza slices should not [should] be served in school because they have little [great] nutritional value.

    *Evidence*: The typical plain pizza slice has 272 calories, 88 of which come from fat. Nearly half of the calories come from carbohydrates, which convert to sugar as part of digestion. The fat content amounts to 9.8 grams, 4.4 of which are saturated. A pizza slice includes 22 mg of cholesterol and 551 mg of sodium, along with 4.1 grams of sugar and 33 grams of carbohydrates. These figures are greatly increased when pepperoni, extra cheese, sausage, and other unhealthy toppings are added.

    *Warrant*:


8.  *Claim*: Fruit juices should [should not] be sold in schools if they contain ingredients other than fruit juice.

**Figure 1–8.** Writing Warrants (*continued*)

*Evidence*: Most fruit juices sold contain such ingredients as water, high fructose corn syrup, citric acid, ascorbic acid, dyes that produce an artificial color, "other ingredients," and 5% fruit juice.

*Warrant*:

9. *Claim*: Pork rinds are [are not] very unhealthy and should not [should] be sold in schools.

   *Evidence*: Pork rinds are typically made from pork skins, pork rinds, salt, lactose, sodium diacetate, salt, malic acid, modified food starch, corn syrup solids, acetic acid, soybean oil, citric acid, sodium citrate, chili peppers, paprika, and monosodium glutamate. For each serving of 1/2 ounce, the consumer ingests 80 calories (45 from fat), 5 grams of fat (2 grams are saturated), 15 mg of cholesterol, and 960 mg of sodium.

   *Warrant*:

10. *Claim*: Focusing gym classes on physical fitness and good health is [is not] a better solution than eliminating all junk food from schools.

    *Evidence*: A school district in Naperville, Illinois, that focused gym classes on teaching students physical fitness, health, and wellness instead of sports skills found that only 3% of its ninth graders were overweight.

    *Warrant*:

## Stage 4B. Language Lesson 2: Identifying Direct Quotes and Information from Sources

Students often don't provide enough information about the source of the direct quotations or paraphrased information they include; they think a parenthetical citation alone is enough. This lesson helps them smoothly incorporate information from sources with appropriate identification.

**EPISODE 4B.1.**  Read the following paragraph:

> Some critics of the plan to test students for alcohol use with the EtG screen argue that the school is encroaching on something that should be the concern of the family. "The concern takes on a zeal that ignores other legitimate concerns such as . . . whether it intrudes on family privacy" (Jones online). All parents have to do to test their child is to walk around the corner to a store and buy a drug test (Jones online). The school doesn't have to be involved. However, the problem with this argument is that unfortunately some families are in denial about alcohol use or uncomfortable talking about it. Parents might feel uncomfortable compelling their child to take a drug test or feel that it's other kids, not their own kids, who are involved in alcohol use. They would most likely applaud the school for helping them with this problem through a plan in which all students are subject to testing, not just their own.

Explain that there is a direct quotation included in the paragraph and other information taken from the article in Figure 1–1. But readers are not given any information about who stated this information and therefore cannot evaluate whether it is valid or credible. Information should be included about the speaker of quotes or the source of other information.

**EPISODE 4B.2.**  Tell students that the following expressions can be used to identify direct quotations and other information from sources. These expressions can be used at the beginning or end of the sentence or in the middle (set off by commas).

According to [name the speaker and his or her position]. . . .

According to [a study by _____ or a report by _____ or an article about _____] . . . .

[Name the person and his or her position] or [Identify the study, report, or article] [states, says, reports, explains, argues, asserts, points out, declares, and so forth] . . . .

Below is a revision of the paragraph that solves the problem. The changes are shown in italics:

Some critics of the plan to test students for alcohol use with the EtG screen argue that the school is encroaching on something that should be the concern of the family. *According to Ed Barocas, legal director of the ACLU of New Jersey,* "the concern takes on a zeal that ignores other legitimate concerns such as . . . whether it intrudes on family privacy" (Jones online). *In addition, Marsha Rosenbaum of the New York–based Drug Policy Alliance points out that* all parents have to do to test their child is to walk around the corner to a store and buy a drug test (Jones online). The school doesn't have to be involved. However, the problem with this argument is that unfortunately some families are in denial about alcohol use or uncomfortable talking about it. Parents might feel uncomfortable compelling their child to take a drug test or feel that it's other kids, not their own kids, who are involved in alcohol use. They would most likely applaud the school for helping them with this problem through a plan in which all students are subject to testing, not just their own.

**EPISODE 4B.3.**  Have students revise the paragraph below (which is based on the information in Figure 1–6) so that the source of direct quotations and other information is clearly explained, in addition to being cited parenthetically:

Even though some schools have been unsuccessful in changing their menus to healthy food options, Aptos Middle School, in San Francisco, has been successful because it has taken student preferences into account. "Students were surveyed about their favorite healthy choices, and based on the results items such as sushi, deli sandwiches, baked chicken with rice, freshly made soup, salads, and fruit desserts were added" ("Junk Food Out" online). "Converting to healthy food choices has increased the profits of Aptos's food service from losing money in 2002 to finishing 2003 more than $6,000 in the black" ("Junk Food Out" online). On the other hand, Berkeley, California, schools, which were not successful, didn't listen to students. "More than 200 students signed a petition protesting the pizza and other new offerings" (Glazer online). Therefore, the Aptos model proves that it is possible for schools to make healthy food attractive to students if they consult students in developing their menus.

## Stage 5. Drafting an Essay

At this point students are ready to begin planning their research paper on whether middle and high schools (or their own school in particular) should eliminate junk food from the cafeteria and vending machines.

**EPISODE 5.1.** Have students, in small groups, use a graphic organizer like those provided in Figures 1–9 and 1–10 to remind themselves of the features of an effective argument, organize their material, and get a sense of the best order in which to present their claims. Because students have already discussed the issue at length, they will have a great deal of information to draw on as they discuss their positions and assemble their evidence.

**EPISODE 5.2.** Using the guiding questions in Figure 1–11, ask your students to help you create a rubric for evaluating their final work. Correlate your specific expectations with their critiques of one another's ideas and writing to this point. The degree to which they must satisfy each requirement depends on their age, their prior experience with this sort of writing, and other factors. Or if there is not time for this activity, they could use the rubric in Figure 1–4 in evaluating their writing.

**EPISODE 5.3.** Have students write the first draft of their research paper. Based on the realities of your classroom and your students' response to your instruction up to this point, decide whether to have them do this in class or as homework and how much time to give them.

**Figure 1–9.** Graphic Organizer 1

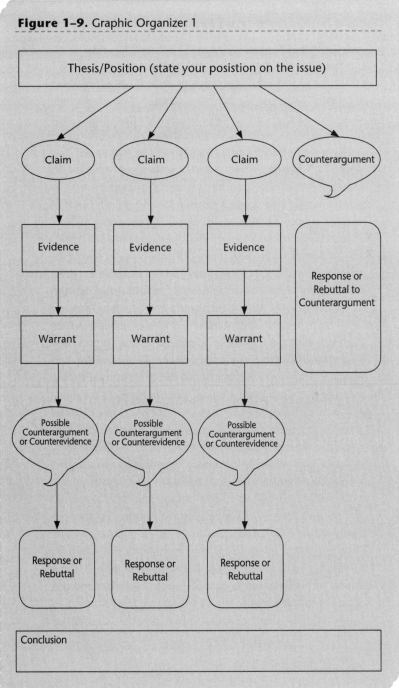

**Figure 1–10.** Graphic Organizer 2

Overall Thesis (position):

**Claim #1:**

   Evidence:


   Warrant:


**Claim #2:**

   Evidence:


   Warrant:


**Claim #3:**

   Evidence:


   Warrant:


**Claim #4:**

   Evidence:


   Warrant:

**Figure 1–10.** Graphic Organizer 2 (*continued*)

**Claim #5:**
Evidence:


Warrant:


**Claim #6:**
Evidence:


Warrant:


**Counterargument or Counterevidence #1:**


**Response or Rebuttal:**


(*continues*)

**Figure 1–10.** Graphic Organizer 2 (*continued*)

**Counterargument or Counterevidence #2:**

**Response or Rebuttal:**

**Other Counterargument or Counterevidence:**

**Response or Rebuttal:**

**Conclusion:**

**Figure 1–11.** Guiding Questions for Evaluating an Argumentation Research Paper

Is the author's overall thesis stated and fleshed out clearly and consistently in the introductory paragraph?

Is the paper organized so that the argument comes across as a series of related claims?

Is each claim clearly related to the overall thesis statement?

Is each claim supported by convincing evidence?

Is the evidence tied to the claim by means of a warrant?

Are counterarguments or counterevidence acknowledged?

Are counterarguments or counterevidence rebutted or responded to in an effective way?

Is there a concluding paragraph that sums up the author's position and that reinforces the overall thesis statement?

Does the paper make sense as a whole, or do some parts veer away from the overall thesis statement?

## Stage 6. Attending to Bibliographic Form

Because students have organized their essays as a series of claims supported by evidence and explained by warrants, their final drafts, for the most part, will consist of a logical sequence of information with appropriate paragraphing. Now it's time to consider how to present citations.

There are a number of options, depending on the discipline. The MLA guidelines (Gibaldi 2003) employed in university English departments and taught by many high school English teachers are customarily used in the humanities. But the social sciences—education, psychology, and other fields that study people rather than texts—follow the recommendations codified in the *Publication Manual of the American Psychological Association* (2001). The *Chicago Manual of Style* (the fifteenth edition was published in 2003) sets out yet another set of rules. And there are countless other grammar and composition textbooks. Rather than learning *the* style for formatting research papers, students are learning *a* style.

Choose an appropriate format and help students understand the conventions you expect. Online sources (e.g., easybib.com) guide students in inputting their information and then provide them with an appropriately formatted list of sources and corresponding parenthetical citations.

## Stage 7. Peer-Group Response and Author Revision

**EPISODE 7.1.** Appendices 1A, 1B, and 1C are examples of research writing students produce after engaging in the kinds of activities described in this chapter. They contain strengths but also some weaknesses. Have your students, in small groups or as a class, use the guiding questions in Figure 1–11 to critique one or more of these examples in preparation for critiquing their own reports.

**EPISODE 7.2.** Have students, in small groups, use the guiding questions in Figure 1–11 to evaluate one another's reports and give and receive feedback on the quality and persuasiveness of their positions. One purpose of this small-group critique is to point out areas in which the evidence is not sufficient to support a claim and suggest additional sources of evidence. Research thus becomes a tool for arguing convincingly rather than a task to be completed in isolation.

**EPISODE 7.3.** Ask students to revise their research paper, seeking new sources of information to support their claims if necessary.

**EPISODE 7.4.** Give students time to make final revisions before submitting their final papers to you. Post their writing in the classroom or on a classroom wiki so that they can read one another's work.

## Extensions

1. Later in the school year, have your students select another controversial, debatable issue to research and then use Figures 1–8, 1–9, and 1–10 to write an argumentation research paper independently. Have them bring their rough drafts to class and, in small peer-editing groups, use the questions in Figure 1–11 to give one another feedback.

2. Have students experiment with other ways of presenting research. They could produce a documentary film on the hazards of eating junk food, create a website that sorts through the critical issues in their topic of interest, develop a work of drama or fiction conveying their perspective on an issue, contribute to web-based listservs and bulletin boards, or speak in public forums.

**Appendix 1A.** "Underage Drinking on Homecoming Night," by Maggie Chung

Controversies have erupted over the issue on whether or not limousine driver Leonel Cesar acted appropriately by calling the police when a group of teenagers from Highland Park High School smuggled alcohol into his luxury vehicle on homecoming night. One of the teenagers even tried offering Cesar money, so he would not call the police. Cesar felt it was his job to be a responsible adult and notified the police. Some of the parents thanked Cesar for what he did while other parents were enraged (Achenbaum, Berger & Black online). Although there are many arguments that can be made on both sides of the story, it can be reasonably concluded that Cesar did the right thing by notifying the police.

Cesar was hired to drive the teenagers to and from the homecoming dance. Before the teenagers were on their way to a restaurant, one of the boys asked Cesar to stop at his house. He came back with a bag that made Cesar suspicious. When Cesar asked what was in the bag, the boy said that it was none of Cesar's business and that he and his friends would tip him well. Cesar concluded that it was alcohol in the bag and notified the teenagers' parents. When he could not get in touch with any parents, Cesar called the police. Some of the teenagers begged Cesar not to call their parents or police by offering him money, but Cesar refused ("Party Bus Driver" online). Those who are against what Cesar did by notifying the police would argue that it is not his business for caring what the students are doing. He should just do his job by providing transportation for the teenagers. The enraged parents said to Cesar, "This is stupid. It's homecoming" (Achenbaum, Berger & Black online). Even though some parents and students were upset because of what Cesar did, they need to look at the situation as a whole. An article states that "teens and parents are forewarned that drinking, smoking, and sex are prohibited in the luxury vehicles" (Achenbaum, Berger & Black online). The Any Time Limo, Inc. Contract also states, "Drinking alcoholic beverages of any type inside our vehicles are prohibited" (online). The teenagers clearly violated the rules and regulations by sneaking in alcohol onto the limousine. As an employee for the limousine company, Cesar needs to enforce the rules with his passengers. He did the right thing by notifying the police when the teenagers refused to obey the rules of the company.

Another point made by the opposition is that the students were smart to hire a limousine service to drive them, so they would not be drinking and driving. It was stated in an article, "Others concede teen drinking is inevitable and credit the Highland Park students for at least hiring someone else to drive" (Achenbaum, Berger & Black online). In New Trier Township, there is a program created to have students pick up their intoxicated peers from parties called "Safe Rides." Jeff Brooks, a volunteer driver for the program, said, "I realize in the real world whatever steps we tried to prohibit kids from drinking don't seem to be working. Our Safe Rides are designed to do one thing: to get kids home safely. It works" (Achenbaum, Berger & Black online). Some of the parents agreed with the opposition. Another article says, "The parents and groups argued the teens did the right thing by hiring a driver to protect themselves and the public's safety while they consumed alcohol" ("Limo Driver Criticized" online). It may seem like a good idea because the teenagers were protecting themselves and other people's safety, but it is giving the teenagers the wrong idea. By allowing the students to hire a limousine service to drive them home while they are intoxicated, it is giving them the idea that they can consume alcoholic beverages whenever they want to and can expect to get home safely afterwards.

Those who do not agree that Cesar did the right thing by calling the police need to realize that the Highland Park High School students are not old enough to be drinking in the first place. The drinking age in the state of Illinois is twenty-one as defined by the Liquor Control Act of 1934. Underage drinking may not be a big deal to some parents. Those parents would argue that if they allow their children to consume alcoholic beverages, then Cesar should not be concerned. The problem is that the parents and students signed a contract with Any Time Limo agreeing to follow all the rules and regulations; one of them being not drinking alcohol in the vehicle ("Any Time Limo, Inc. Prom" online). Cesar was not responsible for being a designated driver to the teenagers because consuming alcoholic beverages is prohibited. Jeff Brooks says in another article,

"I really believe we are saving lives, because we are not losing them." The article also mentions that the program is designed to allow intoxicated high school students get home safely (Malone online). It is true that the "Safe Rides" program is saving teenagers' lives, but it is not fair to those other teenagers who do not drink prior to the age of twenty-one. Teenagers need to take responsibility for their actions instead of relying on nice volunteers to drive them home after they had a night of partying. If they break the law and get caught, they need to face the consequences.

Another point is that students are not allowed to arrive to school being under the influence of drugs or alcohol. The Highland Park High School student handbook states, "Students are prohibited from possessing, using, being under the influence of or distributing alcohol, tobacco, or other prohibited substances in school buildings, on school grounds, in school vehicles or at any school event or activity" ("Alcohol, Tobacco, and Other Drugs" online). Some may say that the teenagers were probably planning to drink the alcohol after the dance, so they would not be near school property to get in trouble for drinking. Even if it was true, the teenagers are displaying bad behavior by disobeying the Illinois state laws and the school policy, and some of the students have already consumed some of the drink prior to the dance. George Fornero, superintendent of Township High School District 113, said, "It doesn't matter if you're driving or someone else is driving. This is unacceptable behavior." School officials said that the intoxicated students were suspended temporarily from athletic and other activities (Achenbaum, Berger & Black online).

If Cesar did not speak up, he would have been in serious trouble if anything happened to one of the teenagers. There are many risks when consuming alcohol such as vomiting, blacking out or passing out, and even dying ("Alcohol Risks" online). Teenagers are inexperienced and so do not know when enough is enough. If anything serious happened to the teenagers, parents would be upset with the driver and the company. According an online blog, "we don't know what the company's contract states as to their liability, but had one of the teens become injured as a result of intoxication, you can bet that one of the teen's parents would have sued the driver and the company" (Stamm online). The opposition may argue that Cesar was hired to provide transportation, not to act as a parent or guardian. If anything happens, it should be the parents' responsibility for allowing their children to drink even though they are not old enough. Even though Cesar was supposed to just provide transportation, he needs to make sure his passengers are following the rules or he would be putting his job on the line. The twenty teenagers had a "we have money so we have power" attitude. Cesar was smart to go against the teenagers' bribe and contact the police. As an adult himself, Cesar should be allowed to intervene when he feels a situation could result in somebody being in danger. Jeff Wagner says in an article, "I'm sorry that some parents are upset that their children received underage drinking citations. . . . Rather than being angry with the limo driver, perhaps those parents should direct ire where it really belongs—namely at their kids!" (online). Parents do not have a reason to be upset with Cesar or Any Time Limo. Instead they should be thankful that Cesar kept their children safe while being under the influence of alcohol.

With many good points that can be made on either side of this issue, it all comes down to the law and doing the right thing. This incident could hurt Any Time Limo's business because of the angry parents, but Alex Mich, the company's general manager, says, "We know we are going to lose some business. It's not about the money; it's about doing the right thing" (Achenbaum, Berger & Black online). The company should be praised for being responsible and reliable. On the bright side, the twenty teenagers are safe thanks to Cesar for intervening and being a responsible adult during the situation. In an article titled "Arrogant, Drunk, and Stupid Is No Way To Go Through High School," the author says, "This whole situation offers a great opportunity for a 'teachable moment'" (Wagner online). Homecoming should be a night filled with great memories, not one that teenagers will regret. Not only do the students learn a good lesson, but the angered parents learned something useful as well. Leonel Cesar did act appropriately towards the situation by not letting the teenagers get away with disobeying the law and by protecting the teenagers from any harm that could have occurred from drinking. It's like that classic quote, "It is better to be safe than sorry."

## References

Achenbaum, Emily S., Susan Berger and Lisa Black. "Debate Swirls Over Arrests of 13 Highland Park Teens Accused of Underage Drinking on Homecoming Night." Chicago Tribune. 8 Oct. 2008. 10 Dec. 2009. www.chicagotribune.com/news /local/chi-teen-limo-drinking-08-oct08,0,3211527.story.

"Alcohol, Tobacco, and Other Drugs." Township High School District 113. 6 Jan 2010. http://www.dist113.org/hphs /RedesignPages/dept_new/deans/student_handbook _2008-09.pdf.

"Any Time Limo, Inc. Contract." 17 Dec. 2009. http://www .anytimelimousine.com/AnyTimeLimo_Transportation Agreement.pdf.

"Any Time Limo, Inc. Prom Regulation." 17 Dec. 2009. http:// www.anytimelimousine.com/prom_agreement.htm.

"Limo Driver Criticized for Drinking Report." United Press International. 8 Oct. 2008. 14 Dec. 2009. www.upi.com/ Top_News/2008/10/08/Limo-driver-criticized-for-drinking -report/UPI-21181223482899.

Malone, Tara. "Program That Offers North Shore Teens a Safe Ride Home Is Up and Running Again." 5 Feb. 2009. 13 Jan. 2010. http://archives.chicagotribune.com/2009/feb/05/local /chi-safe_ridesfeb05.

Mann, Julie. "Limo Driver Turns Down Bribe, Kids Get Busted." WBBM 780. 8 Oct. 2008. 14 Dec. 2009. http://www .wbbm780.com/pages/3102498.php?.

"Party Bus Driver Playing Police or Parent?" Total DUI. 14 Dec. 2009. www.totaldui.com/news/articles/headlines/illinois -underage-drinking-and-driving.aspx.

Stamm, Daniel O. "Teen Drinking Sparks Controversy in Chicago Suburb—What's the Liability?" The Law Blog. 10 Oct. 2008. 14 Dec. 2009. http://lawblog.jpmlaw.net/2008/10/10/limo -liability-dutiful-driver.aspx.

Wagner, Jeff. "Arrogant, Drunk and Stupid Is No Way To Go Through High School." Newsradio 620. 8 Oct. 2008. 16 Dec. 2009. http://www.620wtmj.com/shows/jeffwagner /45157752.html.

**Appendix 1B.** "Following the Aptos Middle School Plan," by Les Poole

Lillian Dickson once said, "Life is like a coin. You can spend it any way you wish, but you only spend it once" ("Life Quotes" online). Are schools spending their coins the wrong way when they fill their cafeterias with junk food or line the hallways with unhealthy vending machines? Aptos Middle School in San Francisco, California seemed to think so and has since replaced unhealthy menu items with wholesome choices. At Aptos, getting rid of junk food "significantly improved student behavior after lunch and reduced litter" ("Junk Food Out" online). Therefore, some people believe that it is a smart decision to completely eliminate junk food in schools. Others believe that it would be more effective to increase exercise and educate children about eating healthy. I fall into the group that believes all schools should follow the Aptos Middle School plan for eliminating junk food.

Aptos Middle School has provided a model that works and should be used as a road map for other schools. After students were surveyed about their favorite choices, the Aptos cafe added popular items such as sushi, deli sandwiches, baked chicken with rice, freshly made soup, salads and fruit desserts. Water, as well as 100 percent fruit juice and milk, replaced all drinks with added sugar, including those in vending machines. Despite widespread parental concerns about junk food available to their kids, school food operations nationwide have been deterred because of the fear that selling junk food is the only way to make money. Also, many of the parents who previously felt forced to pack their students' lunches no longer have to do that because they are confident that their children's lunch money will be spent on a healthy meal. Dana Woldlaw, chair of the Aptos PTSA Student Nutrition Committee said, "It is not enough that our food be less bad for the kids. We want the food to be good for them. Our turkey and roast beef sandwiches are made with lots of fresh lettuce and tomato. The homemade soups are loaded with vegetables. All the juices are 100 percent fruit juice, not 10 percent with added sweeteners. No matter what kids buy for lunch, they are getting something healthy" ("Junk Food Out" online). In addition, kids will enjoy a new beef and cheese piroshki this fall, and chances are they will never miss the eight percent of fat that was removed. The Aptos Middle School plan to eliminate junk food has brought nutritional success to the school.

All schools should follow the Aptos Middle School plan for eliminating junk food because people tend to learn bad eating habits when they are young. Schools can introduce people to healthy food. If not a bad diet can lead to childhood obesity, and other problems caused by unhealthy eating such as poor concentration, tooth decay, and vitamin deficiencies (Newman online). If children are eating grilled chicken, vegetables, and fruit at lunch rather than fried chicken and chips, that will not only have a positive effect on their health, but also their school-work. This is because eating lots of sugary foods makes students less able to pay attention in class or perform well on tests ("Junk Food Should" online). Also, eating to help get rid of stress is a terrible habit that schools would be able to break by switching to a nutritional menu. School is very stressful at times for most students and it is very hard for a lot of students to escape that stress. They feel as if they have no freedom in school except for when they are at lunch and are able to talk to their friends. However, if eating the wrong things becomes a main coping mechanism for stress, it can lead to compromised health, exces-sive weight, and additional stress stemming from the effects. A poor diet can also cause additional stress by leading to blood sugar imbalances that make stressful situations seem even more overwhelming (Scott online). Eliminating junk food from schools would help prevent students from getting into bad eating habits when they are young.

Those who believe that schools should not follow the Aptos Middle School plan argue that kids may need the large number of calories present in unhealthy foods. They argue that teen ath-letes have unique nutrition needs. Because teens work out more than their less-active peers, they generally need extra calories to fuel both their sports performance and their growth. Depending on how active they are, teen athletes need anywhere from 2,000 to 5,000 total calories per day to meet their energy needs ("Eat Extra" online). The problem with this argument is that there are plenty of healthy foods that teenage athletes could eat over the course of a day to boost their calorie intake. Professional athletes don't load up on junk foods to help them get calories or to help them bulk up. As opposed to eating junk food just to fill up on calories, both teen athletes and professional athletes need to eat a balanced diet each and every day. To exercise consistently, one must provide a good supply of high-quality energy to their working muscles. The easiest way to do this is to eat a balanced breakfast and continue eating a variety of high-quality foods throughout the day (Quinn online). The large number of calories present in unhealthy foods are not necessarily a good thing in that they can be counter-productive based on the high levels of fat that are also in these foods.

Another reason all schools should follow the Aptos Middle School plan for eliminating junk food is that obesity causes a number of health problems. Obesity is the condition of being overweight, to the point where a person's health suffers. A lot of increasing problems with obesity in the developed world often start in childhood. Each year obesity-related conditions cost over 150 billion dollars and cause an estimated 300,000 premature deaths in the United States alone ("Health Effects" online). The percentage of overweight and obese people has increased steadily over the years among genders, all ages, all ethnic groups, and all educational levels. Besides an unhealthy appearance, obesity leads to heart disease, diabetes, and strokes. An estimated 70% of diabetes risks in the U.S. can be attributed to excess weight ("Obesity Statistics" online). Overweight and obese conditions are the third leading cause of preventable death in the United States behind smoking and high blood pressure (which is also an effect of obesity). Also, obese youth are more likely to have risk factors for cardiovascular disease, such as high cholesterol. Children and adolescents who are obese are at a greater risk for bone and joint problems, sleep apnea, and social and psychological problems such as stigmatization and poor self-esteem ("Childhood Obesity" online). If junk food is not an option at schools, children will be much more likely to avoid overweight or obese conditions, resulting in an overall much safer and healthier lifestyle.

The other side argues that it would be more effective to increase exercise and educate children about eating healthy. They argue that the way to solve obesity is not to limit the choice of food in schools as children will then load up on unhealthy food outside of schools. They believe that increased exercise along with increased education on eating healthy would be the better alternative (Newman online). The problem with this argument is that children will load up on junk food outside of schools regardless. Although increased exercise and education about eating healthy would help the problem, it wouldn't be enough to completely solve the problem. Any unhealthy food that can be limited to students will end up being beneficial to them. Simply increasing exercise will not be enough to reduce obesity in the U.S. The unhealthy foods that are available to students need to be taken out of school cafeterias and vending machines ("Obesity" online). The most effective plan to reducing obesity would be to both increase exercise and education about eating healthy, as well as eliminating the supply of junk food in schools across the country.

In addition, if soft drinks and other vending machine items are available to kids at schools there is no possible way to prevent them from constantly consuming these unhealthy foods. Therefore, all schools should follow the Aptos Middle School plan for eliminating unhealthy foods and beverages sold in vending machines. The intake of soft drinks account for a large number of health problems related to childhood obesity. Heart disease, diabetes, arthritis and high blood pressure are just a few of the major problems that result from the intake of soft drinks (Nakate online). Vending machines are in 43% of elementary schools and 97% of high schools across the U.S. That is a very dangerous statistic in that researchers have calculated that for each additional soda consumed, the risk of obesity increases 1.6 times ("Ten Facts" online). Besides offering the high-sugar soft drinks, vending machines also offer a number of unhealthy foods. The majority of foods offered in vending machines are packed full of artificial flavoring, sugar, high-fructose corn syrup and preservatives. These nutrient-poor foods can also lead to obesity, diabetes, and a variety of other health related issues (Whittaker online). When given the choice, most students will opt for the less nutritious vending machine selection. Despite the attempt by parents and even some schools to try to promote good health and nutrition, the presence of vending machines stocked full of unhealthy foods undermines attempts at unhealthy guidance. With our lifetime eating habits being determined at an early age, these types of vending machines in schools make it difficult for students to develop healthy eating habits (Whittaker online). The food and drinks that are supplied within vending machines at schools account for an enormous number of health problems that are related to childhood obesity.

However, the other side uses this as their strongest argument. They say that vending machines make a lot of money for the school. The food that is sold in vending machines is aimed at making profits and many of these schools earn as much as $100,000 from vending machine contracts annually (Nakate online). The problem with this argument is that the cost of obesity related problems is much higher than the profits that schools will make. Schools should realize that money comes second to people's lives. Another problem with this argument is that vending machines could be stacked with healthy foods and still make plenty of money annually. At Aptos, school profits even increased after the elimination of unhealthy vending machines and the transformation from junk food to a much healthier menu ("Junk Food Out" online). Vending machines are now available to stock healthy goods too such as fruit and dried foods. Therefore, they can actually be a beneficial item to have inside a school ("Vending Machines" online). Stocking vending machines with healthy choices will not only help reduce a large number of problems related to childhood obesity, but it will also allow schools to continue making high annual profits.

In conclusion, all schools should follow the Aptos Middle School plan for eliminating junk food because of the unhealthy effects that can develop and even lead to death. The other side argued that junk food is where a big chunk of school profits come from. Also, that it is the students' parents to blame for their children's eating habits as opposed to schools themselves. However, the increasing amount of junk food that is appearing in schools undoubtedly has a direct relationship to the increasing amount of people that are becoming overweight or obese every year. Yet schools continue to put their students at a high risk for a number of health problems in their life down the road. By eliminating junk food, Aptos Middle School has provided a model that is successful and that should be followed by all other schools across the country.

### References

"Childhood Obesity." National Center for Chronic Disease Prevention and Health Promotion. 3 June 2010. 11 Jan. 2011. www.cdc.gov/HealthyYouth/obesity/.

"Eat Extra for Excellence." *Teens Health.* 1995-2011. 11 Jan. 2011. http://kidshealth.org/teen/food_fitness/sports/eatnrun.html.

"Health Effects of Obesity." Stanford Hospital and Clinics. 2011. 11 Jan. 2011. http://stanfordhospital.org/clinicsmedServices /COE/surgicalServices/generalSurgery/bariatricsurgery /obesity/effects.html.

"Junk Food Out, Profits In at San Francisco Middle School." Parents Advocating School Accountability. 13 July 2003. 14 Dec. 2010. www.pasasf.org/nutrition/pdfs/profit.pdf\.

"Junk Food Should Be Banned in Schools." 11 Jan. 2011. www.middleschooldebate.com/documents/Junkfood.pdf.

"Life Quotes." 2010. 11 Jan. 2011. www.allgreatquotes.com /life_quotes.shtml.

Nakate, Shashank. "Vending Machines in Schools—Pros and Cons" 16 Dec. 2010. www.buzzle.com/articles/vending -machines-in-schools-pros-and-cons.html.

Newman, Debbie. "Unhealthy Food, Banning From Schools." 6 June 2010. 16 Dec. 2010. http://www.idebate.org/ debatabase/topic_details.php?topicID=760.

"Obesity." Issues and Controversies. 19 June 2007. 5 Jan. 2011. www.2facts.com/icof_story.aspx?PIN=i0900740&term=junk+ food+in+schools.

"Obesity Statistics." Overweight Teen. 11 Jan. 2011. www.overweightteen.com/statistics.html.

Quinn, Elizabeth. "Simple Sports Nutrition Tips." *Sports Medicine.* 14 Dec. 2010. 11 Jan. 2011. http://sportsmedicine .about.com/od/sportsnutrition/tp/SimpleSportsNutrition.htm.

Scott, Elizabeth. "Unhealthy Responses to Stress and How These Bad Habits Affect You." 31 Dec. 2009. 10 Jan. 2011. http:// stress.about.com/od/unhealthybehaviors/a/bad_habit.htm.

"Ten Facts Every Parent Should Know." Parents Against Junk Food. 2006. 5 Jan. 2011. http://parentsagainstjunkfood.org/.

"Vending Machines in Schools." 19 Jan. 2010. 11 Jan. 2011. www.articlesbase.com/electronics-articles/vending-machines -in-schools-1745473.html.

Whittaker, Leslie. "Cons of Vending Machines in Schools." 3 Jan. 2010. 10 Jan. 2011. www.ehow.com/list_5824462_cons -vending-machines-schools.html.

**Appendix** 1C. "Putting an End to Underage Drinking," by Jen Jaroch

"Alcohol remains the substance with the highest rate of use among high school students at 72.5 percent," says a study done in 2009 ("What's New" online). In a classroom of 30, this means 21 of the students have committed the illegal crime of under-age drinking. At these shocking rates, the potential that danger could grasp innocent students is very high, as the youth are very easily influenced. So what can be done? Pequannock Township High School (PTHS) seems to have found a solution: Monday alcohol tests. In addition to their current random drug testing, now the school can detect if alcohol has been consumed since 80 hours earlier (Pignatiello online). Controversy begins to arise under arguments of privacy and false positives. However, these tests will not only protect the students' safety, but guide them in the right direction toward becoming responsible adults. Test-ing for weekend drinking in students at PTHS will be a positive change to help students be safe and succeed.

Not only is underage drinking illegal, it is also very danger-ous. It is well known that alcohol is the leading cause of death among teenagers, while it also contributes to motor vehicle accidents, suicide, and many social and family problems ("Al-cohol" online). This is so significant because young and healthy people are at a great risk of being harmed, especially if drinking is done only over the weekend. Studies have revealed that after not drinking during weekdays, the body has hardly adjusted to a sober system, until it is ambushed with alcohol. "This puts stress on your internal organs in a way that controlled drink-ing on a more regular basis may not. You are also running the risk of passing out and seriously injuring yourself or someone else" ("How" online). Parents should feel confident that their students are in a safe environment at school, because alcohol can not only affect the drinker, but also innocent bystanders. For the students who aren't the innocent ones, alcohol awareness could help them realize that their study-habits are being affected too. Statistics show that children who are drinking alcohol by 7th grade are more likely to have academic problems, substance use, and delinquent behavior in both middle school and high school ("Alcohol" online). Alcohol greatly affects the mind and the body, which would undoubtedly result in destructive actions, including in school. Students who think that weekend drinking won't affect their schoolwork are clearly wrong. After drunken Friday and Saturday nights, the next days "will be spent recovering from a hangover and you won't be giving your body the rest that it needs. Your sleep patterns will be out of sync and you may struggle to sleep properly in the week as well." Insufficient sleep can eventually lead to emotional problems, such as depression. In turn, these unhealthy students may find themselves longing to drink again while under the stress of the school week ("How" online). In order to excel in any part of life, a healthy mind is the first step, which means alcohol cannot play a part.

The school's intention of these tests is to protect the students. As high school administrators are responsible for their students' safety during the school day, it is evident that their greatest concern should be alcohol. Parents trust that the school will do their job to keep adolescents protected. If this means taking random tests to ensure that underage drinking is not occurring, how could parents protest? The superintendent of Pequannock High School, Larrie Reynolds, believes this test will be of great benefit: "We plan to use this new test as part of our comprehensive testing program to keep our kids safe from the dangers of drugs and alcohol" (Bowles online). Reynolds is confirming that the test is not to get the students in trouble or create fear in their lives, but to shelter them from hazardous substances. Two of the biggest jobs of a high school's administration are to ensure students' safety and to instigate the best academic result possible. However, creating intellectual students also means guiding student's study skills and well-being. "Heavy alcohol use in adolescence may lead to alterations in brain structure and function that reduce behavioral (impulse) control, which could, in turn, promote further heavy drinking" ("What's New" online). Administrators cannot just stand by and let these problems occur, for they would not be doing their job. With these tests, students now have a reason to stay home and do homework rather than partying with their friends. They can learn wholesome habits of a normal schedule, getting enough sleep, and keeping their priorities in order. In stopping weekend drinking, it is very probable that academic results would shoot skyward. No matter what the disputes may be, if these tests save the life of just one student, it shouldn't be regretted.

Some protesters may feel unsure about these tests because of statistics, which say that a false positive may result regularly. The EtG test can be so sensitive that it sometimes responds to alcohol coming from soaps, mouthwashes. A writer for *New Scientist Magazine* reports that even, "drinking a sip of communion wine can be enough" (Bowles online). Many complaints come from nurses and doctors who are required to take the tests. When they receive positive results because of simply breathing in vapor from soaps, these nurses have lost their jobs. This leads parents to fear that their children will face similar extreme consequences (Bowles online).

However, something imperative to this controversy is that "under the program, students who test positive will not be kicked off teams or barred from extracurricular activities," says Reynolds ("N. J. School" online). It is worth the risks, because all this test can do is help, not hinder. Instead of expulsion, the students receive *positive* treatment, such as school counseling, and guidance from their parents. For those who have been justly caught drinking, they will learn from professionals the dangers and consequences of underage drinking, and receive help that may be desperately needed. Some students simply need communication to be open in order to get back on track, and this is a perfect opportunity for them. Those who are really in danger may be afraid to confess their wrong-doings, while they truly do desire help. In addition, if a test is truly a false positive, what harm would a few counseling meetings cause? While it could be stressful, it more importantly opens discussion between parents and students, and can even reinforce teenagers to continue not drinking.

Even with self esteem, great social relationships, and good grades, there is one thing all adolescents are susceptible to: peer pressure. Mike Hardcastle, a teen adviser, reasons that "When ugly situations arise and peer pressure kicks in to high gear it is very easy to get caught up in the moment and forget that you will have to live with the choices you make" (online). Especially in high school, it is easy to find students easily influenced and trying to fit in, whether in school or out. While some peer pressure can be positive and supporting good decisions, it can also be very negative, harmful, and particularly serious when it involves teenagers and drinking. Research has found that when peers are involved in alcohol-related decision making, problems greatly increase. Negative consequences have primarily focused on peer influences, parental influences, and alcohol consumption rates (Arata online). That's why schools such as Pequannock find these tests to be beneficial, as they "should be a deterrent to students who feel peer pressure to drink." Reynolds says that the students who deem themselves invincible now have something to stop and think about before they take that sip of alcohol ("N. J. School" online). Is looking cool worth it to make a bad decision? Is it worth it to lose a parent's trust and to face the consequences? If a student would respond yes, they most likely do need professional guidance. Additionally, the students who are regularly persuaded now have back-up as they attempt to turn down alcohol without being teased. As Reynolds says, the new procedure is "going to give our kids riding in the back seat of someone's car a very powerful reason to say no" (Porter online). While adolescents with low confidence or uncertainty are more vulnerable to peer pressure, having strong reasoning to say no can eliminate any doubts, and save many lives.

While students may have been comforted through this program, some parents and their children have begun to worry about privacy issues. Parents may grumble that the school's extreme actions are insinuating that they aren't doing their jobs raising their kids. Some even question the limit that schools will go to in order to control their students. "When will they administer tests to check student's dietary habits?" (Pignatiello online). However, the detail should not be overlooked that while both junk food and alcohol are unhealthy, the latter is *illegal*. Those who oppose the policy have even implied that the school is becoming like a totalitarian government, calling them "Big Brother" (Bowles online). The question that should be asked is whether this is control or duty. Superintendents along with other administrators have a right to make their own decisions on how to protect their students. They are not being a "nanny" as some may complain; they are simply doing their job. Those parents who disagree are also opposing the safety measures that might be necessary. The U.S. Department of Education reports that "four percent of high school students had at least one drink of alcohol on school property during the preceding month in 2009. . . . Alcohol consumption by underage students on school property continues to be a serious concern because it may lead to other crimes and misbehavior" ("What's New" online). A student drinking on school grounds is a dangerous and serious matter that would most likely instill fear into the innocent. One man who opposes states that "there will be an 80 hour period of fear for most high school students on Monday mornings" (Pignatiello online). However, the only reasonable fear would come from their dangerous, drunken peers.

Healthy and clean students don't only help academic results, but it creates major benefits for everyone. A high school well-known for troublesome students will only receive negative recognition, which will keep them from reaching their full potential. Pequannock Township High School is aware of their problem, as they have been "struggling with gaining back the reputation it once had as an academically successful high school, with a promising sports program" (Pignatiello online). In their desperation, extreme measures must be taken immediately to bring back order to their campus. Their new weekend drinking policy will do nothing but bring positive attention to them, opening many doors. There are many opportunities that come from having strong and safe students, such as rewards that come from the National SADD program: Students Against Destructive Decisions. An advertisement reveals that they "awards prizes to schools that are good participants. The top three chapters that collect the most emails . . . will win $100 each month" ("Two" online). Winning money comes with acknowledgement and reinforcement for kids to be reliable role-models. With high expectations, students will be motivated to make goals, because they learn that it pays off. Not only will the tests encourage students, but the positive results will influence other schools, making a nation-wide difference. The US Department of Health and Human Services (DHHS) estimates that 20,000 tests are being performed each month. People who weren't even aware of their dependence pledged to abstinence when they discovered that they have a drink problem (Bowles online). The knowledge of the difference they made is all that some students may need to continue making constructive decisions.

As a dangerous drug, illegal for high school students, alcohol has many dangers that can easily affect vulnerable teenagers. PTHS boldly chose to do something about it. While the policy arose much controversy, the positives that could surface are much more significant. Students' lives, even the innocent ones, may be saved through weekend drinking testing. Now with a reason to say no, the students of PTHS can happily wave good-bye even the thought of underage drinking. Random testing for weekend alcohol consumption will be a positive change to protect students and help them succeed.

## References

"Alcohol and Youth Facts." Apr. 2005. 7 Jan. 2011. www.marininstitute.org/Youth/alcohol_youth.htm.

Arata, Catalina M., Stafford, Jeremy, Tims, Scott M. "High School Drinking and Its Consequences." 2003 Fall. 7 Jan. 2011. http://findarticles.com/p/articles/mi_m2248/is_151_38/ai_113304960/.

Bowels, Claire. "US Teenage Drinkers Face Alcohol Test." 14 Feb. 2007. 3 Jan. 2011. http://www.eurekalert.org/pub_releases/2007-02/ns-utd021407.php.

"How Weekend Drinking Can Turn into a Bigger Problem." 2 Nov. 2009. 6 Jan. 2011. http://www.bukisa.com/articles/185930_how-weekend-drinking-can-turn-into-a-bigger-problem.

"Lead and Manage My School. Preventing Underaged Drinking: A School-Based Approach." 16 Jan. 2008. 11 Jan 2011. http://www2.ed.gov/admins/lead/safety/training/alcohol/index.html.

"N.J. School to Test Students for Weekend Drinking." *USA Today.* 30 Jan. 20017. 3 Jan. 2011. http://www.usatoday.com/news/health/2007-01-30-teen-drinking_x.htm.

Pignatiello, Joe. "High School to Expand Alcohol Testing for Students." 3 Jan. 2011. http://www.helium.com/items/143971-high-school-to-expand-alcohol-testing-for-students.

Porter, David. "High School to Expand Alcohol Testing." 30 Jan. 2010. 13 Dec. 2010. www.komonews.com/news/national/5417466.html.

"Two Chances to Win Big with SADD: How You Can Help." 20 Dec. 2010. 12 Jan. 2011. www.sadd.org/beastbuy.htm

"What's New." 7 Jan. 2011. 10 Jan 2011. www.stopalcoholabuse.gov/.

# Teaching the Research
# Report About Literature

A "literary" research report may explore the connections between a literary work and the author's life, analyze the work's social or cultural milieu, or interpret the work based on evaluations by literary critics. This chapter describes lessons in which students write a research paper exploring the concept of the American dream in John Steinbeck's *Of Mice and Men*. The materials and activities can be adapted for other literary works and other concepts.

## Stage 1. Gateway Activity: Defining the American Dream

The instruction begins by prompting students' interest in the concept of the American dream. Students explore their own knowledge and opinions as preparation for analyzing the concept within a literary work.

**EPISODE 1.1.** Have students, in small groups, complete Figure 2–1, "What Is the American Dream?" Since the groups' rankings and ratings invariably differ, lead a follow-up whole-class discussion in which students debate their views and the meaning of the American dream.

**Figure 2–1.** What Is the American Dream?

**Directions for Part 1:** Rank each of the following statements from the one that *most* expresses the meaning of the American dream (1) to the one that *least* expresses the meaning of the American dream (14):

a. The American dream is the freedom to honestly pursue one's goals.

b. The true meaning of the American dream is laid out in the Declaration of Independence: "We hold these truths to be self-evident, that all men are created equal, that they are endowed by their Creator with certain unalienable Rights, that among these are Life, Liberty and the pursuit of Happiness."

c. The American dream is the ability, through participation in the society and economy, of everyone to achieve prosperity.

d. The American dream is more about spiritual happiness than material goods.

e. Home ownership is the American dream.

f. Being your own boss, having your own business, or becoming rich and famous is the American dream.

g. The American dream is an idea that all people can succeed through hard work and that all people have the potential to live happy, successful lives.

h. The American dream means equal opportunity for all, regardless of race, religion, gender, sexual orientation, and national origin.

i. The American dream is to have all the necessities of life.

j. The American dream is going from rags to riches through thrift and hard work.

*(continues)*

**Figure 2–1.** What Is the American Dream? (*continued*)

k. The American dream is to make do with less and have more time for family, leisure, and volunteering.

l. "Even though we face the difficulties of today and tomorrow, I still have a dream. It is a dream deeply rooted in the American dream. . . . that one day this nation will rise up and live out the true meaning of its creed: 'We hold these truths to be self-evident, that all men are created equal.'" (Martin Luther King, Jr.)

m. The American dream is to live in a bountiful environment with an abundance of land, water, forest, farmlands, wildlife, and wilderness.

n. The American dream is to be able to leave a legacy to future generations after one's death.

**Directions for Part 2:** Indicate the extent to which you agree or disagree with each of the following statements:

1. Anyone who wants to can achieve the American dream.

   ___ *Strongly Agree*          ___ *Somewhat Agree*

   ___ *Somewhat Disagree*    ___ *Strongly Disagree*

2. Working hard is the most important element for getting ahead.

   ___ *Strongly Agree*          ___ *Somewhat Agree*

   ___ *Somewhat Disagree*    ___ *Strongly Disagree*

3. Hard work and determination do not guarantee success.

   ___ *Strongly Agree*          ___ *Somewhat Agree*

   ___ *Somewhat Disagree*    ___ *Strongly Disagree*

4. The American dream is out of reach for some Americans, making it more of a cruel joke than a genuine dream.

**Figure 2–1.** What Is the American Dream? (*continued*)

___ *Strongly Agree*      ___ *Somewhat Agree*

___ *Somewhat Disagree*   ___ *Strongly Disagree*

5. "Nothing can stop the man with the right mental attitude from achieving his goal; nothing on earth can help the man with the wrong mental attitude." (Thomas Jefferson)

   ___ *Strongly Agree*      ___ *Somewhat Agree*

   ___ *Somewhat Disagree*   ___ *Strongly Disagree*

6. "You can have anything you want—if you want it badly enough. You can be anything you want to be, do anything you set out to accomplish if you hold to that desire with singleness of purpose." (Abraham Lincoln)

   ___ *Strongly Agree*      ___ *Somewhat Agree*

   ___ *Somewhat Disagree*   ___ *Strongly Disagree*

7. The American dream is still alive today.

   ___ *Strongly Agree*      ___ *Somewhat Agree*

   ___ *Somewhat Disagree*   ___ *Strongly Disagree*

8. The genes you are born with and/or the environment you are born into can limit your ability to achieve the American dream.

   ___ *Strongly Agree*      ___ *Somewhat Agree*

   ___ *Somewhat Disagree*   ___ *Strongly Disagree*

**EPISODE 1.2.** Have students write about one or two of the statements in part 2 about which they have a strong positive or negative viewpoint. This helps them achieve a deeper understanding of the American dream before they examine it within a literary work.

## Stage 2: Analyzing and Interpreting the Primary Source

**EPISODE 2.1.**   Have students read *Of Mice and Men*, by John Steinbeck. Ask them to look for the various characters' views of the American dream. As they read, have them, individually or in small groups, complete the chart in Figure 2–2. Periodically lead a whole-class discussion of these characters' views of the American dream—what it means to them, whether they see it as achievable, what they see as obstacles to achieving it, whether their conception of it changes, and so forth.

You may need to include other activities to ensure that students understand the novel. You might have students research the setting (time period and location), note any questions they have as they are reading, research the Robert Burns poem "To a Mouse" to which the title alludes, make connections between the Burns poem and the novel, and so forth.

**EPISODE 2.2.**   After students have finished reading the novel, ask them what they think Steinbeck is saying about the American dream through the characters and events. Encourage them to present evidence and warrants to support their views. Have them discuss their ideas in small groups or as a whole class or both.

## Stage 3: Researching Critical Controversies

Students usually write a better research paper about a work of literature when they participate in critical conversations—when they examine differing viewpoints, debate them, and argue a position. As Gerald Graff and Cathy Birkenstein explain, "Experienced writing instructors have long recognized that writing well means entering into conversation with others. Academic writing in particular calls upon writers not simply to express their own ideas, but to do so as a response to what others have said" (2006, ix). Help students enter this conversation by identifying aspects of a work that are the subject of debate by literary critics. (Frame the debate in terms your students will understand.)

**Figure 2–2.** *Of Mice and Men* and the American Dream

Explain what the American dream is or means to each of the following characters.

| Character | WHAT IS THE CHARACTER'S DEFINITION OF THE AMERICAN DREAM? WHAT DOES THE CHARACTER SAY OR BELIEVE ABOUT THE AMERICAN DREAM? | FIND QUOTATIONS FROM THE NOVEL THAT REVEAL THE CHARACTER'S DEFINITION AND VIEWS OF THE AMERICAN DREAM. |
|---|---|---|
| George | | |
| Lenny | | |
| Candy | | |
| Crooks | | |
| Curley's wife | | |

One controversy related to *Of Mice and Men* is whether the ending is optimistic or pessimistic. Some critics argue that the ending is optimistic, that Steinbeck is suggesting that the characters have overcome obstacles and are on their way to attaining the American dream. Others argue that the ending is pessimistic, that Steinbeck is suggesting that attaining the American dream is impossible for many.

**EPISODE 3.1.**   Figure 2–3, Critical Viewpoints: *Of Mice and Men* and the American Dream, contains excerpts from six critical commentaries on the novel. Ask students, individually or in small groups, to read these critical viewpoints. Have them answer the following questions about each source:

- Does the writer/do the writers think Steinbeck is optimistic or pessimistic about the potential for achieving the American dream?

- How do you know?

- What reasons and/or evidence does the writer/do the writers give to support this view?

**Figure 2–3.** Critical Viewpoints: *Of Mice and Men* and the American Dream

"Readers of *Of Mice and Men* have argued about whether the ending is bleak and fatalistic (that is, that George will now just become like all the rest of the lonely 'boys' and grow old, poor, and dispensable like Candy and Crooks) or whether it is hopeful (that George and Slim will now forge a friendship that will allow them to aspire to a better life). Regardless of how one interprets the conclusion, which Steinbeck leaves mysterious and unspoken, the story . . . is an affirmation of the qualities of 'our species' to rise above base nature."

— *Claudia Durst Johnson, in* Understanding Of Mice and Men, The Red Pony, *and* The Pearl: A Student Casebook to Issues, Sources, and Historical Documents *(p. 19), published in 1997 in Westport, CT, by Greenwood Press.*

**Figure 2–3.** Critical Viewpoints: *Of Mice and Men* and the American Dream (*continued*)

"The fact that the setting for *Of Mice and Men* is a California valley dictates, according to the symbolism of Steinbeck's landscapes, that this story will take place in a fallen world and that the quest for the illusive and illusory American Eden will be of central thematic significance." (p. 145)

"The dream of George and Lennie represents a desire to defy the curse of Cain and fallen man—to break the pattern of wandering and loneliness imposed on the outcasts and to return to the perfect garden. George and Lennie achieve all of this dream that is possible in the real world: they are their brother's keepers. Unlike the solitary Cain and the solitary men who inhabit the novel, they have someone who cares. The dream of the farm merely symbolizes their deep mutual commitment, a commitment that is immediately sensed by the other characters in the novel. The ranch owner is suspicious of the relationship, protesting, 'I never seen one guy take so much trouble for another guy.' . . . The influence of George and Lennie's mutual commitment, and of their dream, has for an instant made these crippled sons of Cain their brother's keepers and broken the grip of loneliness and solitude in which they exist." (pp. 146–47)

"The death of the dream, however, does not force *Of Mice and Men* to end on the strong note of pessimism critics have consistently claimed. For while the dream of the farm perishes, the theme of commitment achieves its strongest statement in the book's conclusion. Unlike Candy, who abandons responsibility for his old dog and allows Carlson to shoot him, George remains his brother's keeper without faltering even to the point of killing Lennie while Lennie sees visions of Eden. In accepting complete responsibility for Lennie, George demonstrates the degree of commitment necessary to the Steinbeck hero, and in fact enters the ranks of those heroes." (p. 148)

(*continues*)

**Figure 2–3.** Critical Viewpoints: *Of Mice and Men* and the American Dream (*continued*)

"[I]t should be noted that this novel about man's loneliness and 'apartness' began with two men—George and Lennie—climbing down to the pool from the highway and that the novel ends with two men—George and Slim—climbing back up from the pool to the highway. Had George been left alone and apart from the rest of humanity at the end of the novel, had he suffered the fate of Cain, this would indeed have been the most pessimistic of Steinbeck's works. That George is not alone has tremendous significance. In the fallen world of the valley, where human commitment is the only realizable dream, the fact that in the end as in the beginning two men walk together causes *Of Mice and Men* to end on a strong note of hope—the crucial dream, the dream of man's commitment to man, has not perished with Lennie." (p. 149)

— Louis Owens, "Of Mice and Men: *The Dream of Commitment"*
*(pp. 145–49) in* John Steinbeck, *edited by Harold Bloom,*
*published in New York in 1987 by Chelsea House.*

"One aspect of the dream that George repeatedly describes to Lennie also needs scrutiny. . . . The dream not only gives a direction to their lives, but also makes them feel different from other people. Since this sense of difference can mean little to Lennie, it is part of the consolation George receives from the dream. George wants to be superior. With Lennie gone, his claim to distinction will be gone. Thus when George shoots Lennie, he is not destroying only the shared dream. He is also destroying the thing that makes him different and reducing himself to the status of an ordinary guy. . . . This is a story not of man's defeat at the hands of an implacable nature, but of man's painful conquest of this nature and of his difficult, conscious rejection of his dreams of greatness and acceptance of his own mediocrity." (pp. 134–35)

—Warren French, *in the article* "Of Mice and Men: *A Knight
Dismounted and a Dream Ended" (pp. 130–37) in*
Readings on John Steinbeck, *edited by Clarice Swisher,*
*published in 1996 in San Diego, CA, by Greenhaven Press.*

**Figure 2–3.** Critical Viewpoints: *Of Mice and Men* and the American Dream (*continued*)

"All the characters in the novel are living lies. Curley knows his marriage will never work out but will not admit it. His wife knows there never was a show business career for her, but she will continue to tell the story at the drop of a hat. George knows that he will never have a farm of his own, but he keeps talking himself and Lennie into it. And Candy knows his dog cannot live without his constant care and that he also needs constant care to survive." (p. 43)

"By losing Lennie, George becomes just like any other man. . . . However, this tragedy offers a glimmer of hope. George is not walking off a total loner—he is walking off with Slim. Just two ordinary men walking off, but together. . . . Both Slim and George are very understanding men, and they are sensitive to what has just happened. They are not fictional dreamers, the kind George pretended to be for Lennie's sake. Perhaps their dream of owning a farm is more realizable now that they have formed a phalanx and accepted their status as average men." (pp. 46–47)

— *Gerald Newman and Eleanor Newman Layfield, from* A Student's Guide to John Steinbeck, *published in 2004 in Berkeley Heights, NJ, by Enslow Publishers, Inc.*

"In *Of Mice and Men*, Steinbeck presents [his] philosophy through the eventual negation of George and Lennie's dream, which is taken away by the events occurring in their life, the things that happen to them to show the dream, or end, to be merely a fantasy. *Of Mice and Men*'s major theme of naturalism . . . is consistent with the philosophy of the author and the scientist.

"Naturalism is the idea that the scientific facts of heredity and environment are the forces controlling human existence, and neither human will nor divine assistance can alter the course determined by heredity and environment. Both forces are clearly functioning in *Of Mice and Men*.

(continues)

**Figure 2–3.** Critical Viewpoints: *Of Mice and Men* and
the American Dream (*continued*)

George and Lennie are bindlestiffs because that is the class worker to which they belong by the facts of their birth, their potential, and the socioeconomic circumstances of their environment. Their attempts to change the circumstances are shown to be impossible."

—*Cynthia Burkhead, from* Student Companion to John Steinbeck *(pp. 58–59), published in Westport, CT, in 2002 by Greenwood Press.*

"Was Lennie's death at George's hand the inevitable outcome of events, or did George have other choices? In spite of Slim's approval ['You hadda, George. I swear you hadda' *OMM*, 107], it is obvious that George was acting willfully when he killed Lennie: he did not have to kill his partner; he chose to do so. Though one could argue that George took Carlson's Luger in order to protect himself and Lennie against the advances of the mob, such speculation seems unlikely.

"It is far more reasonable to assume that George planned to shoot Lennie as soon as he discovered that Lennie had killed Curley's wife. By killing Lennie, George consciously decides to give his friend the only protection available to him. With the fatal pistol shot, George rationalizes that he has sent Lennie off to the dream farm forever. By the time George walks away from the grove with Slim, he has let go of the escape dream for himself as well and has embraced the competing dream of living without Lennie and just being one of the guys. . . . [Steinbeck] makes one thing very clear: George's pulling the trigger is a reaction to the voices of a cruel reality from which neither he nor Lennie can escape any longer."

—*Charlotte Cook Hadella, from* Of Mice and Men: A Kinship of Powerlessness *(pp. 62–63), published in 1995 in New York by Twayne Publishers.*

**EPISODE 3.2.** After students have examined the different viewpoints presented in the excerpted critical articles, have them use Figure 2–4 to analyze the arguments on each side of the controversy. Encourage them to include any points and evidence they have thought of in addition to what they have found in the critical articles.

## Stage 4: Drafting a Literary Research Paper

**EPISODE 4.1.** Have students use Figure 2–5 to plan and organize their ideas for writing. When they have finished, quickly check their work to be sure everyone is on the right track. Meet individually with any students who are struggling, or have them work with a peer.

**EPISODE 4.2.** Have students write a draft of their paper and bring it to class for peer review. Ask them, in small groups, to use the guidelines in Figure 1–11 (see Chapter 1) to review one another's writing: has the writer summarized the critical controversy, taken a position, developed strong, logical arguments with evidence and warrants, and effectively addressed counterarguments and counterevidence?

**EPISODE 4.3.** Review effective ways to incorporate quotations from sources, both primary and secondary (see Stage 4 in Chapter 1) and an appropriate bibliographic form for citing sources that students reference in their papers (see Stage 6 in Chapter 1).

**EPISODE 4.4.** Encourage students to revise their writing based on the feedback from their group.

**EPISODE 4.5.** When students have completed their papers, provide a forum in which they can share their writing (a classroom wiki or website, for example) and thus extend the critical conversation. You can also extend the critical conversation by having students exchange papers with students in another class or at another school, read them, and write responses.

**Figure 2–4.** Analyzing the Arguments

Literary critics have presented opposing interpretations of John Steinbeck's *Of Mice and Men*. Some argue that the novel is pessimistic and that it suggests that for some people the American dream is impossible to achieve. Others argue that ultimately the ending of the novel is optimistic and that the novel suggests that the American dream is achievable for George and others like him. What are the claims and/or evidence on each side of this issue?

| THE ENDING IS OPTIMISTIC, SUGGESTING THE POSSIBILITY OF ACHIEVING THE AMERICAN DREAM. | THE NOVEL IS PESSIMISTIC, SUGGESTING THE IMPOSSIBILITY OF ACHIEVING THE AMERICAN DREAM. |
| --- | --- |
| | |

**Figure 2–5.** Planning and Organizing

Introduction summarizing the interpretive debate (what are the different viewpoints, who is taking what positions, and what are their arguments?):

Your thesis (position on the issue stated in Figure 2–4):

What is your first argument (claim) in support of your position?

*Evidence from OMM:*

*Warrant:*

*Evidence from OMM:*

*Warrant:*

What is your second argument (claim) in support of your position?

*Evidence from OMM:*

*Warrant:*

*Evidence from OMM:*

*Warrant:*

*(continues)*

**Figure 2–5.** Planning and Organizing (*continued*)

What is your third argument (claim) in support of your position?

*Evidence from OMM:*

*Warrant:*

*Evidence from OMM:*

*Warrant:*

What is one argument made by one of the critics *on the other side* of this issue?

What evidence does this critic use to support his or her argument?

What is your response or rebuttal to this argument (be sure to include evidence and warrant)?

What is another argument made by another one of the critics *on the other side* of this issue?

What evidence does this critic use to support his or her argument?

What is your response or rebuttal to this argument (be sure to include evidence and warrant)?

**Figure 2–5.** Planning and Organizing (*continued*)

If applicable, what is another argument made by another one of the critics *on the other side* of this issue?

What evidence does this critic use to support his or her argument?

What is your response or rebuttal to this argument (be sure to include evidence and warrant)?

Conclusion:

## Extensions

1.  Have students write a research paper on another literary work. Ask them to find a point of disagreement in the critical literature about the work and write an argument taking a position on the issue.

2.  Ask students to evaluate a work of literature in relation to its historical period. How did Thoreau represent a Transcendentalist perspective? Was Richard Wright a Realist or a Naturalist? How accurate is Shakespeare's portrayal of thirteenth-century society in Verona and Mantua in *Romeo and Juliet*?

3.  Let students experiment with other ways of presenting research: produce a media slide show or a website that sorts through the critical issues in a literary work, contribute to web-based listservs and bulletin boards, speak in public forums.

# What Makes This a Structured Process Approach?

As we hope we have demonstrated in the pages of this book, we believe that kids learn best when actively engaged in activities that interest them. This is the foundation of a structured process approach. Now that you have seen what teaching this way looks like, we'll lay out the basic principles that guided our planning and that might guide yours, too, going forward:

- The teacher usually identifies the task, such as writing an argumentation research paper, although students may participate in deciding what they want to learn how to write. Even with the task identified, students often begin learning the processes involved by participating in familiar activities such as debating whether cell phones should be allowed in school or whether junk food should be removed from school cafeterias and vending machines.

- Learning begins with *activity* rather than with the product of that learning. For example, the instruction in Chapter 1, rather than beginning with a model research report, begins with an activity in which the teacher stages a debate with a student about a controversial issue. The lessons in Chapter 2 begin with an activity in which students, in small groups, rank a series of opinions about the American dream.

- The teacher designs and sequences activities that allow students to move through increasingly challenging problems of the same type. In the instruction in Chapter 1 students are first given an article about a school that is testing all students for alcohol use within the past three days. Students share their views and chart the arguments in favor of the testing and those opposed to it. Then they compose written arguments supporting their viewpoint, that incorporate claims, evidence, and warrants. In another series of activities they research junk food in school, examining several sources and collecting information based on their own observations. Again, they chart the opposing arguments, formulate their own positions, gather and analyze additional evidence, and develop arguments with claims, evidence (data), and warrants.

- Students' learning is highly social, involving continual talk with one another as they learn procedures and strategies for particular kinds of writing. Throughout structured process instruction, students participate in whole-class and small-group discussions as they grapple with various research-related problems and writing activities.

- The teacher designs the activities that take students through the particular writing process that produces the final product. However, in class, *the students are the ones talking and doing.* After helping the students identify the elements of an argumentation research report, the teacher has students apply these procedures to increasingly difficult research concepts and issues. The teacher's role is primarily to help students apply the strategies, not exercise a heavy hand in leading discussions and guiding the writing.

A structured process approach therefore places the teacher in the role of designer and orchestrator of student activity through which the *students themselves* make many of the decisions about how to write and how to assess the quality of their writing. Figure 3–1 is a more comprehensive list of principles that guide this approach. We and other teachers influenced by George Hillocks have outlined this approach in a number of publications, including Hillocks (1975, 2006), Hillocks, McCabe, and McCampbell (1971), Johannessen, Kahn, and Walter (1982, 2009), Kahn, Walter, and Johannessen (1984), Lee (1993), McCann, Johannessen, Kahn, Smagorinsky, and Smith (2005), Smagorinsky (2008), and Smagorinsky, McCann, and Kern (1987). Several of these titles are available for free download at www.coe.uga.edu/~smago/Books/Free_Downloadable_Books.htm.

**Figure 3–1.** Principles of a Structured Process Approach

1. Instruction allows students to develop procedures for how to compose in relation to particular kinds of tasks. The processes that students use to write argumentation research reports, for example, are different from those used to write personal narratives.

2. Because different tasks require different procedures, writing instruction cannot rely solely on general strategies. Rather than simply learning "prewriting" as an all-purpose strategy, students learn how to prewrite in connection with a specific genre—writing a research report, for example, in which case, small groups of students might brainstorm debatable issues they could research.

3. With writing instruction focused on specific tasks, students work toward clear and specific goals with a particular community of readers in mind. A research report arguing that schools should eliminate junk food could be addressed to school officials who will be making decisions about school policy, or it might be addressed to students to motivate them to create a healthy school environment. A research report arguing for eliminating junk food in schools could be addressed to an audience that is highly skeptical of any "nanny state" policies that eliminate students' (or their parents') personal rights and freedoms. Each readership requires attention to different rhetorical features and interpersonal issues in order to be convinced of the writer's position.

**Figure 3–1.** Principles of a Structured Process Approach (*continued*)

4. Even with clear and specific goals, thinking and writing are open-ended. Students operating from different assumptions can take opposing perspectives in arguing their viewpoint. Students typically disagree about whether junk food should be allowed in school or whether Steinbeck's *Of Mice and Men* makes an optimistic or pessimistic statement about people's ability to achieve the American dream.

5. Composing is a highly social act, rather than the work of an individual. Students discuss their compositions with peers at every stage of development. In a structured process approach, people learn to write by *talking* as well as by writing.

6. The teacher identifies the criteria used to assess the writing. Students often help develop these evaluative criteria by discussing what they value in the writing they read. When the writing is tied to large-scale assessment, such as writing essays for a district or state gateway exam, the criteria may already be in place.

7. The teacher *scaffolds* students' learning of procedures by designing activities and providing materials that the students may manipulate. Initial instruction is simple and manageable. For example, when learning how to write research reports, students might first explore a limited amount of information about alcohol testing in schools. Instruction then progresses through more challenging aspects of the writing, such as synthesizing information from a number of sources and addressing counterarguments and counterevidence. Attention to form comes later in the instruction when students have developed content to write about, rather than earlier, as is often the case with instruction in how to write the five-paragraph theme.

8. When possible, the teacher provides additional readerships for students' writing, such as having the students post their writing in the classroom or on a classroom wiki or submit their writing to a contest, the school newspaper, the school literary magazine, and so on.

# Designing Structured Process Instruction

A structured process approach to teaching writing involves two key ideas: *environmental teaching* and *inquiry instruction* (Hillocks 1986).

## Environmental Teaching

One important assumption that underlies environmental teaching is the belief that *each task we ask students to do involves unique ways of thinking*. For example, think of what is involved in three types of writing tasks: defining what is and is not junk food, comparing and contrasting the nutritional value of two snacks, and writing an argument about whether schools should eliminate junk food. Each relies on different ways of thinking and communicating one's thinking in writing. An environmental approach, then, stresses learning particular sets of *procedures* for engaging in specific sorts of *tasks*.

To help students learn to accomplish a new task, a teacher needs to involve students directly in developing strategies for undertaking that task. In other words, the teacher introduces activities that will help students learn *how* to do this new kind of thinking and writing.

A task in this sense involves both *doing* something and *thinking about how it's done* so that it can be done again with different materials. A task, then, may comprise writing a personal narrative, or comparing and contrasting similar yet different things, or arguing in favor of a solution, or defining a complex concept such as progress or success. Our goal for students is that when they complete this task, they are able to repeat the process more independently next time.

## Inquiry Instruction

Inquiry is the particular structure through which students work, often in collaboration with one another.

Again, the teacher plays a strong role designing activities that provide the basis for students' inquiries into the problems they investigate. For research reports, the problem may be *how* to generate claims, evidence, and warrants and *how* to anticipate and respond to opposing arguments.

The students play with materials related to the questions they hope to settle through their writing. *Play* in this sense refers to experimenting with ideas. For example, let's say students are going to read and research a novel focusing on the concept of the American dream. In order to be able to examine this concept within a literary work, they first need to think about their own understanding and views about the American dream: What is it? What are its features and attributes? What does it mean to others? Are others' views justifiable or valid?  To help them examine this concept, the teacher might have students form groups and decide whether they agree or disagree with a set of statements about the American dream ("Home ownership is the American dream," "The American dream is more about spiritual happiness than material goods," etc.). As students interact in groups, the teacher encourages them to experiment with "what if?" questions (Is it possible to be poor and have achieved the American dream?).

Students' work is open-ended in that the activities may have many plausible solutions or outcomes. Some students may argue that if people work hard they can achieve the American dream. Others may argue that not all people can achieve the American dream because of discrimination (not being allowed to marry the person they want, for example). Small-group discussions allow students to play with these ideas and try out solutions that may or may not ultimately figure into the final decision.

## Applying Structured Process Instruction

This book illustrates how you might put these principles into practice when teaching students to write argumentation research reports on a debatable issue (whether schools should eliminate junk food in the cafeteria and vending machines, for example). It also illustrates how to write a research paper that takes a position on a critical debate about a literary work, such as whether Steinbeck's *Of Mice and Men* is optimistic or pessimistic about man's potential for achieving the American dream. Some of the writing focuses on literature, while some focuses on writing across the curriculum.

By deliberately working through the various stages required to complete an immediate product, your students have an opportunity to write research reports that matter to them and to convey their views to others. The process of producing these reports contributes to their understanding of their experiences. By making the procedures explicit, they will be able to apply them to other situations involving research writing when they work independently. Students address a particular problem, work with specific problem-solving strategies, and rehearse their compositions in discussions with other students before they put their ideas on paper. Instruction is grounded in students' authentic need to "argue to learn": to exchange views as a way to grow intellectually and more clearly understand who they are and what they believe.

## What Can You Expect When Teaching Writing with This Approach?

The approach outlined in this book reveals how the process of preparing students to write well-developed, thoughtful research reports is time-consuming for both teachers and students. The detailed, systematic process sequences students' progress through procedures related to both thinking and writing about the problem. The activities cannot attend to *all* the considerations in completing a task as complicated and interactive as writing. Realistically, before students are able to apply specific skills and strategies to new situations, they will need several experiences and appropriate feedback from you, from other students, and, if possible, from other readers. But with continual reinforcement, the procedures that students generate should enable them to write strong research reports on future occasions when they choose or are called upon to create them.

## Where Do You Go from Here?

This book and the others in this series provide specific plans you can adapt to your own teaching; they also introduce you to a process you can use to design original instruction based on your classroom and your students' needs. The guide below will help you design writing instruction using a structured process approach:

1.  *Identify the task that will form the basis for your instruction.* Assuming that any general process such as "prewriting" differs depending on the demands of particular writing tasks, identify the task that will form the basis of the instruction. This task might be specified by a formal writing requirement and assessment provided by a mandate from the school, district, or state (e.g., argumentation); it might be writing that you believe is essential in your students' education (e.g., research reports); it might be writing that students identify as something they want to learn how to do (e.g., college application essays); or it might come from some other source or inspiration.

2.  *Conduct an inventory of students' present writing qualities and needs.* With the task identified, you will probably want to see what students' writing of this sort looks like prior to instruction. Doing so allows you to focus on students' needs and avoid teaching strategies they already know. You could take this inventory by providing a prompt like, *Write an argument in which you attempt to persuade a person or group of people to adopt your position on an issue that is important to you.* Then assess their abilities in relation to your *task analysis*, below.

3.  *Conduct a task analysis.* Either by consulting existing sources or by going through the processes involved in carrying out the writing task yourself, identify what students need to know in order to write effectively according to the demands of readers. The task analysis should treat both *form* (e.g., the presence of a claim, evidence, and warrant) and *procedure* (e.g., how to generate evidence and warrants or how to anticipate opposing arguments and respond to them). The task analysis will also help you identify the evaluative criteria that you ultimately use to assess student work.

4.  *Conduct an activity analysis.* Determine the types of activities that will engage students with materials that are likely to foster their understanding of the processes involved in the task. Identify familiar and accessible materials they can manipulate (e.g., issues currently being debated in the school, community, or nation) for the early stages of their learning, and more complex materials (e.g., information about junk food in schools or the views of various critics writing about *Of Mice and Men* and the American dream) for subsequent activities.

5.  *Design and sequence students' learning experiences so that they provide a scaffold.* Design increasingly challenging tasks of the same sort using increasingly complex materials. Sequence these activities so that students are always reiterating the process but doing so in the face of greater challenges. The activities should present continual opportunities for students to talk with one another as they learn the processes involved in carrying out the task.

6.  *Consider opportunities to teach language usage in the context of learning procedures for task-related writing.* Specific kinds of writing often benefit from particular language strategies. For example, students need to learn ways to identify the source or speaker of direct quotations and other information. Targeting language instruction to specific instances of its use helps overcome the problem inherent in discrete grammar instruction, which is that it fails to improve students' understanding of how to speak and write clearly.

7.  *Relying on the task analysis, develop rubrics through which students clearly understand the expectations for their writing.* These rubrics may be developed in consultation with students, adopted from established criteria such as those provided for state writing tests or advanced placement exams, adopted from model rubrics available on the Internet, created by examining a set of student work that represents a range of performance, and so on.

8.  *Provide many opportunities during the learning process for feedback and revision.* Students should be given many occasions to get feedback on drafts of their writing. This feedback can come by way of peer response groups, your written response to their writing, writing conferences with you, or other means.

## A Structured Process Approach and Professional Learning Communities

Currently many school faculties constitute a professional learning community made up of collaborative teams. Structured process instruction is particularly effective in this context. Teachers together develop instruction and analyze student work. Teams use the student writing produced during the instructional sequence as a basis for discussing what worked, what students are struggling with, and what should be done differently or what needs to be added. They collaboratively design rubrics for scoring student work so that expectations for students are consistent. Collecting data on student performance from pretest to final product allows the group to evaluate student growth, reflect on the strengths and weaknesses of the instruction, and plan future classroom activities.

Our own teaching has shown us that this approach can greatly improve students' writing over the course of instruction. We look forward to hearing how you have adapted this approach to your own teaching and helped your students learn how to use written expression to meet their responsibilities as students, writers, friends, communicators, and citizens.

## Questions for Reflection

1.  What current events or issues in the nation or your community might you use to interest your students in writing research reports?

2.  What possibly interesting topics would be problematic? What guidelines could students use to determine topics to avoid?

3.   What topic would be a good alternative to the junk
     food issue in Chapter 1? What sources/information (like
     those in Figure 1–6) would you develop for students to
     examine and analyze? What critical controversy would
     be a possible alternative to the one in Chapter 2 based on
     *Of Mice and Men*? What sources/information (like those
     in Figure 2–3) would you develop for students to examine
     and analyze?

4.   The sources students use must be reliable and valid. What
     activities could you develop to help students learn how
     to evaluate the validity of the sources they find on the
     Internet and elsewhere?

5.   In what ways in addition to those suggested in this book
     could technology be incorporated to help students learn
     to write research reports?

6.   What are the characteristics of an effective introduction
     and conclusion in a research report? What activities
     could you develop to help students who are struggling
     with writing effective introductions and/or conclusions?

7.   This book includes minilessons on writing warrants and
     on ways to identify the speaker or source of direct quota-
     tions and other information. What other specific diffi-
     culties related to language usage and conventions might
     your students encounter when writing a research report?
     What minilessons could you develop to help them?

8.   What particular difficulties might English language
     learners and struggling readers face when writing a
     research report? What activities could you develop or
     what adjustments would you make to help them?

9.   What activities could you develop to help students
     reflect on the thinking and writing processes they use in
     creating a research report?

10. What kinds of comments on student drafts will be most helpful? What kinds of comments will be least helpful? What guidelines could you develop to help you provide the most helpful comments you can? What specific comments would you make to help the writers of the sample student papers included in Chapter 1?

# References

Burkhead, Cynthia. 2002. *Student Companion to John Steinbeck*. Westport, CT: Greenwood Press.

*The Chicago Manual of Style*, 15th ed. 2003. Chicago: Univ. of Chicago Press.

French, Warren. 1996. "*Of Mice and Men*: A Knight Dismounted and a Dream Ended." In *Readings on John Steinbeck*, Ed. Clarice Swisher. San Diego, CA: Greenhaven Press.

Gibaldi, J. 2003. *MLA Handbook for Writers of Research Papers*, 6th ed. New York: Modern Language Association.

Graff, Gerald, and Cathy Birkenstein. 2006. *They Say, I Say: The Moves That Matter in Academic Writing*. New York: W. W. Norton.

Hadella, Charlotte Cook. 1995. *Of Mice and Men: A Kinship of Powerlessness*. New York: Twayne Publishers.

Hillocks, G. 1975. *Observing and Writing*. Urbana, IL: National Council of Teachers of English. Retrieved December 6, 2008 from www.coe.uga.edu/~smago/Books/Observing_and_Writing.pdf.

———. 1986. *Research on Written Composition: New Directions for Teaching*. Urbana, IL: National Conference on Research in English and Educational Resources Information Center.

———. 2002. *The Testing Trap: How State Writing Assessments Control Learning*. New York. Teachers College Press.

———. 2006. *Narrative Writing: Learning a New Model for Teaching*. Portsmouth, NH: Heinemann.

Hillocks, G., B. McCabe, and J. McCampbell. 1971. *The Dynamics of English Instruction, Grades 7–12*. New York: Random House. Retrieved August 4, 2006 from www.coe.uga.edu/~smago/Books/Dynamics/Dynamics_home.htm.

Hillocks, G., E. Kahn, and L. Johannessen. 1983. "Teaching Defining Strategies as a Mode of Inquiry." *Research in the Teaching of English* 17: 275–84.

Johannessen, L. R., E. Kahn, and C. C. Walter. 1982. *Designing and Sequencing Pre-writing Activities*. Urbana, IL: National Council of Teachers of English. Retrieved July 2, 2008 from www.coe.uga .edu/~smago/Books/Designing_and_Sequencing.pdf.

———. 2009. *Writing About Literature, 2d Edition, Revised and Updated*. Urbana, IL: National Council of Teachers of English.

Johnson, Claudia Durst. 1997. *Understanding* Of Mice and Men, The Red Pony, and The Pearl: *A Student Casebook to Issues, Sources, and Historical Documents*. Westport, CT: Greenwood Press.

Kahn, E., C. C. Walter, and L. R. Johannessen. 1984. *Writing About Literature*. Urbana, IL: National Council of Teachers of English.

Lamm, K. 1998. *10,000 Ideas for Term Papers, Projects, Reports and Speeches*, 5th ed. New York: Macmillan.

Larson, R. 1988. "The High School 'Junior Theme' as an Adolescent Rite of Passage." *Journal of Youth and Adolescence* 17: 267–83.

Lee, C. D. 1993. *Signifying as a Scaffold for Literary Interpretation: The Pedagogical Implications of an African American Discourse Genre*. Urbana, IL: National Council of Teachers of English.

McCann, T. M., L. R. Johannessen, E. Kahn, P. Smagorinsky, and M. W. Smith, eds. 2005. *Reflective Teaching, Reflective Learning: How to Develop Critically Engaged Readers, Writers, and Speakers*. Portsmouth, NH: Heinemann.

Newman, Gerald, and Eleanor Newman Layfield. 2004. *A Student's Guide to John Steinbeck*. Berkeley Heights, NJ: Enslow Publishers, Inc.

Owens, Louis. 1987. "*Of Mice and Men*: The Dream of Commitment." In *John Steinbeck*, Ed. Harold Bloom. New York: Chelsea House.

*Publication Manual of the American Psychological Association*, 5th ed. 2001. Washington, D.C.: American Psychological Association.

Smagorinsky, P. 1991. "The Writer's Knowledge and the Writing Process: A Protocol Analysis." *Research in the Teaching of English* 25: 339–64.

———. 2008. *Teaching English by Design: How to Create and Carry Out Instructional Units*. Portsmouth, NH: Heinemann.

Smagorinsky, P., T. McCann, and S. Kern. 1987. *Explorations: Introductory Activities for Literature and Composition, Grades 7–12.* Urbana, IL: National Council of Teachers of English. Retrieved December 8, 2008 from www.coe.uga.edu/~smago/Books /Explorations.pdf.

Smith, M. W. 1989. "Teaching the Interpretation of Irony in Poetry." *Research in the Teaching of English* 23: 254–72.

Steinbeck, John. 1937, 1965. *Of Mice and Men.* New York: Penguin.

Toulmin, S. E. 1958. *The Uses of Argument.* New York: Cambridge University Press.

Toulmin, S. E., R. Rieke, and A. Janik. 1984. *An Introduction to Reasoning,* 2d ed. New York: Macmillan.

# Teaching Students to Write

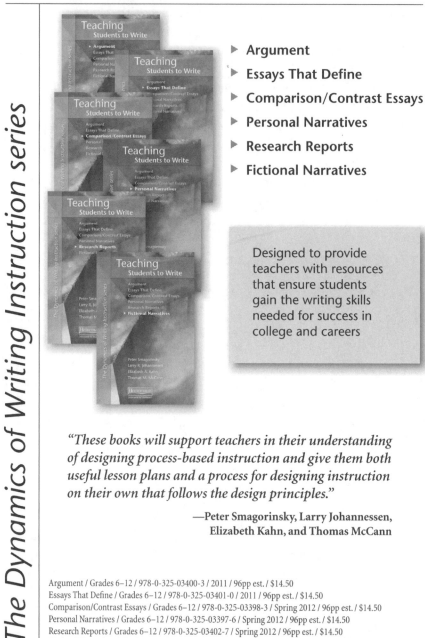

*The Dynamics of Writing Instruction series*

- ▶ **Argument**
- ▶ **Essays That Define**
- ▶ **Comparison/Contrast Essays**
- ▶ **Personal Narratives**
- ▶ **Research Reports**
- ▶ **Fictional Narratives**

Designed to provide teachers with resources that ensure students gain the writing skills needed for success in college and careers

*"These books will support teachers in their understanding of designing process-based instruction and give them both useful lesson plans and a process for designing instruction on their own that follows the design principles."*

—Peter Smagorinsky, Larry Johannessen,
Elizabeth Kahn, and Thomas McCann

Argument / Grades 6–12 / 978-0-325-03400-3 / 2011 / 96pp est. / $14.50
Essays That Define / Grades 6–12 / 978-0-325-03401-0 / 2011 / 96pp est. / $14.50
Comparison/Contrast Essays / Grades 6–12 / 978-0-325-03398-3 / Spring 2012 / 96pp est. / $14.50
Personal Narratives / Grades 6–12 / 978-0-325-03397-6 / Spring 2012 / 96pp est. / $14.50
Research Reports / Grades 6–12 / 978-0-325-03402-7 / Spring 2012 / 96pp est. / $14.50
Fictional Narratives / Grades 6–12 / 978-0-325-03399-0 / Spring 2012 / 96pp est. / $14.50

Heinemann
DEDICATED TO TEACHERS

**CALL 800.225.5800** WEB **Heinemann.com** FAX **877.231.6980**